ARISE, GO.

TAKE YOUR PLACE
IN THE SPIRITUAL BATTLE

Crystal L. Ratcliff

Arise, Go.

Take Your Place in the Spiritual Battle

Crystal L. Ratcliff

Crystal Ratcliff
WRITING FOR HIM

A SPECIAL THANKS

As with all my writing projects, I rely on several sweet friends to partner with me in prayer. Many of them also contributed to the study by being content and line editors. I so appreciate their part in this ministry. They are always willing to give me thoughts and feedback on my writing, as well as pray for me when writing gets difficult.

Thank you, my special friends: Denise, Erica, Jodi, Rachel, and my pastor's wife, Mrs. Twila Jones.

I also want to thank my husband, Marc, who has been my biggest supporter over the years. He is always ready with prayers and an encouraging word. He also challenges me to continually grow spiritually. I am grateful for the opportunity to serve the Lord with him, my best friend.

Finally, I want to thank my social media followers who have been on this journey with me. I'm so thankful for their constant support, encouragement, and prayers. It truly is a blessing to me!

TABLE OF CONTENTS

INTRODUCTION

Many years ago, the Lord used a series of messages from the Book of Joshua to change my life. My pastor at that time preached about the crossing of the Jordan River as being a picture of crossing over into the Victorious Christian Life. The Lord used those messages to draw me into a closer relationship with Him— one that was so rewarding and fulfilling that I determined in my heart to never go back.

I never wanted to go back to the dry, empty Christian life I had been living. I never wanted to go back to going through the motions of Christianity. I never wanted to go back to a life without experiencing true peace and everlasting joy.

Of course, I found the decision I had made was really only a small step in my journey with the Lord. I soon learned that while I never wanted to "go back," it would take diligent, continual effort to maintain a right relationship with the Lord. It would take daily, consistent time with the Lord in His Word and prayer. It would take being obedient to His Word and surrendering my will. It would take a choice—over and over again.

Years later, the Book of Joshua still holds a special place in my heart. I've studied it several times since that first time so many years ago, and each time, the Lord reveals more spiritual lessons for my life. I hope to share some of those lessons with you as we study the Book of Joshua together.

Joshua, along with the children of Israel, will take us on the journey into the Promised Land. They experienced many battles, great victories, and yes, even some defeat as they conquered and possessed the land. Studying their journey will take us on a spiritual journey of our own filled with application for our everyday lives. Now where do we begin?

"Now after the death of Moses the servant of the LORD it came to pass, that the LORD spake unto Joshua the son of Nun, Moses' minister, saying, Moses my servant is dead; now therefore **arise, go** over this Jordan, thou, and all this people, unto the land which I do give them, even to the children of Israel."

Joshua 1:1-2

Arise, go.

It sounds simple enough, but this command was the beginning of a step of faith that would become a lifelong journey for the children of Israel. The previous generation had refused to enter the Promised Land despite the urging of Joshua and Caleb (Numbers 13-14). Their fear and lack of faith left them wandering in the wilderness for forty years. This new generation, the "little ones" (Numbers 14:31), whom God had promised to bring into the land now looked to Joshua to lead them.

They were comfortable in the wilderness. They had probably grown accustomed to wandering. God had provided for their every need, from clothes and shoes that never "waxen old" (Deuteronomy 29:5) to manna from heaven (Exodus 16:15). Possessing the Promised Land was going to take work. They would have to leave what was comfortable and easy, enter into battles to conquer the land, and step out in obedience to possess it for themselves.

Arise, go.

As I studied through Joshua this time, I found that command wasn't fulfilled with the crossing of the Jordan. It wasn't fulfilled with any one of the many battles the children of Israel faced. It wasn't even fulfilled in the final chapter as Joshua charges the children of Israel and encourages them to "...choose you this day whom you will serve..." (Joshua 24:15).

Arise, go.

It's a command that continues for the life of every believer. We are called to a deeper relationship with the LORD, a closer walk with Him. We cannot allow anything—sin, fear, unbelief, comfort, etc.—to hold us back from moving forward with God. We must leave the familiar behind, trust the LORD for our future, and step out in obedience. We must arise, go, and take our place in the spiritual battle.

Before You Begin

Before you start chapter one, let me explain how this study is organized. I purposely do not divide my chapters into daily lessons because I do not know how much time you are able to commit to your daily Bible study. We are all in different seasons of life. Some of you are squeezing your devotions into naptimes or between chasing little children. Some of you may have a set amount of time before you race out the door for work each day. Some of you are able to carve away extended time to spend with the Lord on a daily basis. I would recommend you take it slow and prayerfully seek what the Lord wants to show you through this study. Let Him lead you to spend more time on some chapters if needed. Each chapter includes sections that might be perfect break points for you. I've also included a suggested schedule of Bible reading and study in Appendix C if you are looking for a little more structure.

One final note before you begin, each chapter will end with a section called "Armour Up." As we study, you will learn that the only offensive weapon in our spiritual battles is the Word of God. We must know God's Word and how to use It to be effective in the battles we face. "Armour Up" will include a passage of Scripture for you to study on your own by reading, defining terms, looking up cross references, and/or doing a Scripture writing. Make this space your own and seek what the Lord wants to teach you through the study of His Word!

CHAPTER ONE
MEET THE CAPTAIN

Text: Joshua 1

We will follow Joshua throughout this study, much like the Children of Israel followed him into the Promised Land. We can learn a lot just by the meaning of his name. Joshua means "The Lord is Salvation" or "Jehovah Saves." His name actually corresponds with the name of Jesus found in Matthew 1:21, "…and thou shalt call his name JESUS: for he shall save his people from their sins."

Joshua is a picture of Christ, the commander who led his people to deliverance and victory, and Jesus is the Captain of our Salvation. Before we look into that amazing parallel, let's dig into Joshua's history and get to know him a little bit more. Look up the following verses and record what you learn about Joshua:

Exodus 17:9-16

Exodus 24:9-18; 32:15-19

Arise, Go.

Numbers 13:1-14:10

Numbers 27:15-23

Deuteronomy 1:38

Deuteronomy 3:21-29

Deuteronomy 31:7-8

Deuteronomy 34:9

Consider Joshua's character traits. What do you find most admirable? What traits did he have that would be advantageous as we prepare for battle?

In what ways did the LORD prepare Joshua to become the commander of the people?

As I studied these verses, I first took note of Joshua's position as Moses' minister. This role put him in the place to see great and mighty things right alongside Moses. Can you imagine having a front row seat as God demonstrated His glory over and over again? It would have been absolutely amazing! No wonder Joshua became known for his courage and faith as one of the two spies ready and willing to enter into the Promised Land.

I also noticed how the LORD was preparing Joshua for the role as commander all along. In the role as Moses' minister Joshua learned how to be a servant, not only to Moses, but also the LORD (Joshua 24:29). He learned how to be a skilled warrior and rely completely on the LORD for victory (Exodus 17:9-16). After the triumph over the Amalekites, God commands Moses to write it in a book and "…rehearse it in the ears of Joshua" (Exodus 17:14). God used Moses to exhort him, encourage him, and strengthen him in preparation for leading the people and dividing the land.

GOD IS ALWAYS PREPARING US FOR WHAT HE HAS PREPARED FOR US.
~Elisabeth Elliot

Later in the study, we will discuss how important it is to take time to remember. For now, take some time to consider all the ways the LORD has prepared you for this present time.

The Captain of our Salvation

While Joshua was chosen to be the commander of the Israelites and lead them into the Promised Land, we have an even more perfect commander who has done everything necessary to provide a way of salvation for us. Jesus, the Captain of our Salvation, not only made the arrangements for us to have an eternal home in heaven, but He leads us on our journey home.

Look up "captain" in the Websters 1828 dictionary and record the definition here:

Take some time and read through Hebrews 2:6-18. Use the space provided to summarize and/or record what stands out to you in this passage:

I am certainly not an expert on the rank of captain in our military, but I was able to find some information that I found interesting and applicable to us for spiritual application. The first thing that caught my attention was the size of the company a captain would be responsible for commanding. The army explains that a company would be made up of 3-5 platoons totaling between 60 to 200 soldiers. According to Britannica, "a captain is the commander of the largest group of soldiers that an officer can be expected to know *personally*." Aren't you thankful that while the number of Christian soldiers far surpasses two hundred, our Captain knows each of us personally?

Now take a look at some of these action words that are used when describing the responsibilities of a captain. As you read them, consider how they might apply to Jesus, the Captain of our Salvation, and what He has done and continues to do for us.

Organize and Plan	Teach and Train	Provide Necessities

Record Keeping	Command

Lead	Serve	Encourage and Reward

Our Captain, Jesus Christ, made all the arrangements and preparation between here and heaven. The arrangements have been made, but each individual is responsible for accepting the free gift of salvation. John 3:16 says, "For God so loved the world that he gave his only begotten Son, that whosoever believeth in him should not perish, but have everlasting life."

We are all sinners (Romans 3:10, 23; 5:12). We are hopelessly lost and have "earned" death—eternal separation from God. Our hope is found in the gift of Jesus Christ alone (Romans 6:23; 5:8; Ephesians 2:8-9). We accept that gift by admitting we are sinners in need of a Savior, believing on Jesus Christ—His death, burial, and resurrection—and calling on Him for salvation (Romans 10:9-10, 13).

Has there been a time in your life when you accepted Christ as your Personal Savior?

If so, write out a brief salvation testimony in the space provided. It is always good to keep your salvation experience fresh in your mind. It is our best witnessing tool!

IF YOU ARE UNSURE OF YOUR SALVATION, PLEASE TAKE TIME TO READ MY TESTIMONY IN APPENDIX B

Now that we can trust the Lord has made all the arrangements for us from here to heaven, let's continue to look at the ways that He acts as our Captain in our everyday lives. The Captain of our Salvation gives commands and blesses our obedience to those commands. He leads the way. He is with us in the battle, guiding our steps as we journey through this life. Our Lord and Savior encourages us with promises from His Word. He delights in rewarding us and desires to say, "Well done, thou good and faithful servant:" (Matthew 25:21).

When we truly grasp the role that Jesus has as the Captain of our Salvation, two questions asked in a sermon by Charles Spurgeon must be answered:

Why do we act as if we have no Captain?

Why do we worry when everything is in the Captain's care?

The reason we struggle to rest in the Captain's care is because we often let the "what ifs" of this world take hold in our hearts and minds. However, "…there is one glorious *if* that will kill them all, it is this, — *if* the Lord Jesus Christ could fail, — *if* he could desert us, then all would be lost. That kills all the other *ifs*, because it is an impossible *if*. He cannot fail us or leave us; he must live; he must conquer; and while that is the case, the other *ifs* do not signify anything to us" (Spurgeon, 1882).

We must put the "what ifs" behind us if we are going to answer the call to *arise and go* in our Christian lives. We must believe that everything is in our Captain's care and trust Him to lead and guide us as we move forward with Him.

Armour Up*: I Peter 5:5-11

*see page iv for directions, continue on next page if needed.

Arise, Go.

CHAPTER TWO
KEYS TO SUCCESS

Text: Joshua 1

It's time to prepare for battle.

When we make any decision to advance our relationship with the LORD, we can expect a battle to ensue. The enemy we face may be the devil or this present world, but often we are in the midst of an intense battle against our very own flesh (Romans 7:14-25). As we make the decision to *arise and go*, it is important for us to know and understand the keys to our success.

Write Joshua 1:8 in the space below and begin thinking about what kind of success is mentioned here. By the way, this is the ONLY place the word success is used in the Bible.

The Armour of God

We will come back to Joshua 1:8 later in the chapter, but for now let's turn our attention to what will likely be a familiar passage, Ephesians 6:10-18. This passage is one of my favorites, and I never tire of hearing lessons and sermons taught and preached about the Armour of God. I even covered it in one of my previous studies, *There's a Fly in my Tea!*. As we will see, this passage holds all the keys to success for our spiritual battles, and it takes a concentrated effort—and decision—to put on this vital armour on a *daily* basis.

Take some time to read and study Ephesians 6:10-18. I have included it below with extra spacing so that you will be able to "mark it up" freely. Define terms using Websters 1828 Dictionary or Strong's Concordance. Underline, circle, highlight. Take time to look up cross references. Make this study your own!

Ephesians 6:10-18

[10] Finally, my brethren, be strong in the Lord, and in the power of his might.

[11] Put on the whole armour of God, that ye may be able to stand against the wiles of the devil.

¹² For we wrestle not against flesh and blood, but against principalities, against powers, against the rulers of the darkness of this world, against spiritual wickedness in high places.

¹³ Wherefore take unto you the whole armour of God, that ye may be able to withstand in the evil day, and having done all, to stand.

¹⁴ Stand therefore, having your loins girt about with truth, and having on the breastplate of righteousness;

¹⁵ And your feet shod with the preparation of the gospel of peace;

¹⁶ Above all, taking the shield of faith, wherewith ye shall be able to quench all the fiery darts of the wicked.

¹⁷ And take the helmet of salvation, and the sword of the Spirit, which is the word of God:

¹⁸ Praying always with all prayer and supplication in the Spirit, and watching thereunto with all perseverance and supplication for all saints;

The first thing I notice is that we are unable to fight the battle on our own. All too often, I attempt to lean on my own strengths, talents, and abilities to help me through a situation. I am sure I don't need to tell you how that usually ends—frustration and failure. Instead, we are told to "be strong in the Lord, and in the power of his might" (vs. 10). It takes more than physical strength and abilities to fight a spiritual battle, and it is only through His strength and power that we are able to succeed.

We are told to "Put on the whole armour of God..."(vs. 11) and "...take unto you the whole armour of God..." (vs. 13). We must choose to put on the armour. We must make the effort to put it on, fasten it with prayer, and stay in the battle. There can be no turning back. Once we have accepted Christ as Savior, we are a target of the enemy. He wants to destroy us and our testimony for Christ. The armour allows us to "be able to stand against the wiles of the devil" (vs. 11). The word *stand* means to continue safe and sound, stand unharmed, to stand ready and prepared, and to be of a steadfast mind.

IF WE DISTRUST EITHER OUR CAUSE, OR OUR LEADER, OR OUR ARMOUR, WE GIVE HIM (SATAN) AN ADVANTAGE.

·Matthew Henry

In Ephesians 6:12, we are reminded that our fight is not against "flesh and blood," or humanity. If we aren't careful, we may see those on this earth who are working against the cause of Christ and pushing ungodly agendas as our enemies. We must remember that our fight is not with them. It is with the principalities, powers, rulers of darkness, and spiritual wickedness, all of which are working on behalf of Satan. Our enemy is smart and cunning. His tactics and devices are specifically designed for our weaknesses. The armour of God allows us to *withstand*—stand against, oppose, or resist—Satan's attacks (vs. 13). James 4:7b assures us, "Resist the devil, and he will flee from you."

Now let's take a closer look at that armour. Use the space provided to record some notes about the pieces of the armour and/or verses listed and answer the questions.

BELT OF TRUTH – The ancient soldier's loins, or waist, was girt about with a leather belt which held the other armour pieces in place. How would this correlate with a "belt of truth" in our Christian armour?

Why would the Belt of Truth be listed first?

What does it protect us from?

Psalm 119:142, 151, 160

II Timothy 2:15

II Timothy 3:16-17

BREASTPLATE OF RIGHTEOUSNESS – The breastplate was a metal shield protecting the vital organs of the body, especially the heart. Consider this shield in our spiritual armour.

What does the Bible say about our hearts (Proverbs 4:23 and Jeremiah 17:9)?

What would the Breastplate of Righteousness protect us from?

Define *righteousness*:

Whose righteousness would we be putting on (Romans 3:10, Titus 3:5, Philippians 3:9)?

GOSPEL OF PEACE – Soldiers must protect their feet, and the instruction given here is that our feet be "shod with the preparation of the gospel of peace." This represents our firm foundation.

What allows us to have peace with God (Romans 5:1, Ephesians 2:14-22)?

A Christian wearing shoes prepared with the gospel of peace is free from anxiety and fear in the battle. We are confident and willing to advance against the enemy.

(Ratcliff, 2016)

Why would having a firm foundation in the Gospel of Peace be necessary for us in the battle?

What is the best way we can advance against our enemy? HINT: Matthew 28:19-20

SHIELD OF FAITH – Roman soldiers carried massive shields, nearly four feet long by three feet wide. It was meant to protect and deflect attacks from the enemy, just as our shield of faith is to "...quench all the fiery darts of the wicked" (vs. 16).

"Our shield of faith is based on *Who* God is, not on *what* He is doing" (Ratcliff, 2016). We can stand strong in faith, trusting the Lord as He is at work in our lives.

What is the definition of faith in Hebrews 11:1?

What are some of the fiery darts Satan uses against you (i.e. worry, doubt, anger, etc.)?

Read and consider Psalm 18:1-3.

HELMET OF SALVATION – "No soldier would go into battle without a helmet, and Christian soldiers are no different" (Ratcliff, 2016). We must protect our minds!

Read I Thessalonians 5:8. What does it call the helmet in this verse?

Why would having a "hope of salvation" be important for protecting our minds?

When we remember the hope we have in salvation, it helps us keep an eternal focus. Our minds will be fixed on the Truth of

God's Word and things which are pleasing to Him. We won't spend time considering the lies from Satan that cause us to doubt, worry, and fear. We will rest in the hope and peace we have through Jesus Christ our Lord.

How do we go about putting on the helmet of salvation?

Romans 12:1-2

Philippians 2:5

Philippians 4:6-9

II Corinthians 10:5

SWORD OF THE SPIRIT – After we put on the armour, we must pick up our only offensive weapon. God's Word is our only weapon against Satan's attacks.

Hebrews 4:12

Have you ever considered that Satan knows God's Word too? He twists God's Word and causes us to question and doubt. He will use our weapon against us if we let him. We must know God's Word and put It into practice if we are going to use It effectively in the battle.

PRAYING ALWAYS – We cannot forget this important instruction for the Christian soldier. Without prayer, our armour would be incomplete.

While this is listed last in the passage, it is the most important piece of our armour. You could say it fastens all the other pieces together. We cannot be successful in putting on any piece of the armour or using our weapon without the help of prayer.

Note the words always and all in verse 18. What does the use of these words tell you about the importance God puts on prayer?

Define watch (vs. 18).

Who are we instructed to pray for in verses 18-20?

We must pray for one another. We must pray for those in ministry. Satan would like nothing better than to destroy Christians, their families, and their churches. He is "like a roaring lion" searching for someone who is alone and discouraged, vulnerable to attack (I Peter 5:8). The LORD can and will bring people alongside to encourage us, and we should be ready and willing to do the same for others. In Joshua 1:16-18, the people encourage Joshua with the same words God used to encourage him, "...be strong and of a good courage." We must watch and pray!

The Offensive Weapon

Now let's go back to our text and look more closely at Joshua 1:8, "This book of the law shalt not depart out of thy mouth..."

Take time to define the following words (use Webster's 1828 Dictionary and/or Strong's Concordance) and take a few notes from the verses listed.

Depart

"...but thou shalt meditate therein day and night..."

Meditate

Psalm 1:2

Psalm 119:15

Psalm 119:48

"...that thou mayest observe to do according to all that is written therein..."

Observe

Psalm 119:34

Deuteronomy 5:1

Deuteronomy 6:17

John 14:15

Read Joshua 1:7. Note we are instructed to "turn not from it to the right hand or to the left." This is a caution not to veer off course – even a degree will set me on a course that leads me far from where God wants me to be.

"...for then thou shalt make thy way prosperous, and then thou shalt have good success."

Prosper

Success (Strong's Concordance)

Psalm 1:1-3

Summarize the keys to Biblical success and prayerfully consider any areas in need of improvement.

Armour Up: Psalm 19:7-11

Arise, Go.

CHAPTER THREE
DEAL WITH THE PAST

Text: Joshua 2

This chapter feels like a bit of an interruption to the story of the children of Israel entering into the Promised Land, but there are some valuable lessons here for us. We must deal with the past before we are able to *arise and go* with God. Let's take a look at what we can learn from Joshua and Rahab.

I imagine it took some courage for Joshua to send out spies after his previous experience spying out the land. After all, Joshua and Caleb had tried to convince the people to have faith and trust the LORD, but the evil report of the other men convinced the people to rebel against the LORD (Numbers 13-14). They refused to enter the land and the consequence was wandering 40 years in the wilderness and death for those who had murmured against the LORD. Can you imagine Caleb and Joshua watching and waiting for 40 years?

Joshua was encouraged over and over to "be strong and of a good courage" (Deuteronomy 31:23; Joshua 1:6, 9, 18). This mighty warrior needed that encouragement—not because he feared going into battle, but more likely because he understood the weight and responsibility of leading God's people and the fear of failure.

Now we see only two spies being sent to spy out Jericho. Spend a few minutes reflecting on their experiences.

Spies in the Promised Land (Numbers 13-14)	Spies in Jericho (Joshua 2)

This time the spies brought back a favorable report. They declared, "Truly the LORD hath delivered into our hands all the land; for even all the inhabitants of the country do faint because of us" (Joshua 2:24). Joshua must have been relieved to hear the LORD had prepared the way for them, and the people would be encouraged to follow him into the Promised Land.

Joshua didn't let his past experience stop him from moving forward in obedience. He didn't let his fears stop him from taking a step of faith by sending those spies to Jericho. His past did not become a stumbling block to the future God had planned for him.

If we are not moving forward in our relationship with the LORD, it's only a matter of time until we are moving backward. One of Satan's favorite tactics is to use doubt and fear to keep us frozen in a state of inaction. If we are dwelling on past mistakes and what we *perceive* as failures, we will never be ready and willing to move forward with God's plan for our lives.

IF WE ARE NOT MOVING FORWARD IN OUR RELATIONSHIP WITH THE LORD, IT'S ONLY A MATTER OF TIME UNTIL WE ARE MOVING BACKWARD.

We will make mistakes.

We will fail.

It is how we respond that matters. Do we surrender to discouragement and defeat? Or do we see those times as an opportunity for us to learn and grow?

I started writing over 20 years ago and was excited to publish my first novel. After several rejection letters, a small publisher offered to work with me. I believed it was the Lord's leading and signed the contract. I was thankful to have my book "out there," but I quickly realized I had much to learn about writing and the publishing industry. I started connecting with other writers, joined writing communities, and became involved in critique groups designed to "hone my craft." My writing developed and improved so much that I began to look at that first book with a bit of embarrassment. Truthfully, my best works of fiction remain unpublished.

Looking back on that experience, I could consider it a failure. Instead, I can see how God used that time in my life to prepare me for the writing ministry He has for me today. If I had let doubt and fear keep me from moving forward with my writing, I would have missed opportunities to grow in my personal walk with the LORD and share that with others.

We are continually called to move forward with God. He may be asking that we simply *arise and go* in our daily walk with Him, taking simple steps of obedience and faith. He may be calling us to leave our comfort zones behind and *arise and go* over into that Victorious Christian Life I mentioned in the introduction (if you haven't read it yet, you really should 😊).

Is there a past experience(s) that causes you to doubt or fear moving forward with God?

Rahab

While Joshua could have let his past experience hold him back, it was Rahab's own personal sin that could have kept her from following the LORD. Thankfully, she did not let her title of a "harlot" define who she was or who she could become in God's eyes.

Rahab expressed great faith for someone who would not have been in the position to sit under the teaching of God's Word. She was a Gentile woman, abiding in one of the most wicked cities of that time. She had heard of the Israelites and their defeat over Egypt and the parting of the Red Sea. She knew they served the God in heaven. She said, "…for the LORD your God, he is God in heaven above, and in earth beneath" (vs. 11).

After hiding the spies and deceiving the servants of the king of Jericho (this is reported, not condoned), Rahab negotiated her safety and the safety of her family in the upcoming battle. The spies agreed to her request, but they instructed her to hang a scarlet line out her window and to bring all her family into the house. Only those within the house would be guaranteed safety.

How is this similar to the Passover (Exodus 12:7, 12-14)?

All too often, Christians are allowing sins of the past to keep them from moving forward with God. Fornication. Adultery. Abortion. Divorce. Addiction. Satan wants Christians to carry those sins (and many more) forever, placing an agonizing burden upon them that will keep them discouraged and defeated, and eventually lead to their destruction.

Yet the Bible is filled with examples of God's mercy and forgiveness. Take, for instance, David. We can probably all quickly recall at least one of his most heinous sins – the adultery with Bathsheba and the murder of her husband, Uriah the Hittite, to cover up that sin. When confronted with his sins, David repented and sought the LORD's forgiveness (II Samuel 11-12).

What does Nathan tell David the LORD has done with his sin in II Samuel 12:13?

Read Psalm 103:8-12. What comfort do you find in these verses regarding the LORD's mercy and our sins?

Toward the end of David's life, he was able to sing a song of praise in II Samuel 22. This song is a close parallel to Psalm 18. It was probably written after Saul died and when David took the throne as King of Israel *before* his well-known sin of adultery and murder. While the song may have been written earlier in his life, David was still able to look back and sing the song again as he considered his whole sin-filled life.

Take some time to prayerfully read II Samuel 22. What words or phrases stand out to you as evidence that David believed he had been forgiven of any and all past sins?

Why do you think David was able to sing these words and phrases to the LORD despite his history?

I'm always fascinated by what I call "one-liner" testimonies in the Bible. Sometimes these are an unexpected break in genealogy, such as "Achar, the troubler of Israel" (I Chronicles 2:7) and "Enoch walked with God" (Genesis 5:22). Other times, it is how someone is described or known. David is known as a man after

God's own heart (I Samuel 13:14; Acts 13:22). These "one-liners" always make me consider what would be said about me. How would God sum up my life?

Even after accepting Christ as our Savior, we will never live a sinless life. There will be times when we sin. It is our response to our sin that matters.

It was David's response to his sin that allowed him to maintain the testimony of being "a man after God's own heart" despite his failures. Each time David was confronted with sin, he demonstrated godly sorrow and Biblical repentance.

What is the difference between godly sorrow and worldly sorrow?

What elements of godly sorrow and Biblical repentance can you identify in David's response to his sin (see Psalm 51, II Samuel 12, I Chronicles 21)?

David's life gives us hope that when sin is dealt with Biblically, God takes away the guilt. He was able to sing that song of praise at the end of his life because he had truly repented of his sin and accepted the LORD's forgiveness. This is what allowed David to still be used by God in great and mighty ways.

Now let's look back at Rahab again. We don't know much about her life following the account in Joshua. As promised, she and her family were saved from the destruction of Jericho and she dwelled in Israel (Joshua 6:17, 25). Every time we see Rahab mentioned in Scripture, she is identified as "the harlot" except in one very important place.

Read Matthew 1:1-17 (spelled Rachab vs. 5). What is Rahab known for in this passage?

Why do you think it is significant that Rahab is listed in the genealogy of Christ?

What other women do you find in Christ's genealogy and what do you know about them (use cross references if needed)?

What does the mention of these women in Christ's genealogy tell you about God's power to forgive, restore, and use those who have a "messy" past?

We must not allow Satan to hold past sins over our heads, making us feel guilty. God never intended for us to live defeated and discouraged by sin. He sent Jesus to give us victory over sin! We can move forward in our lives and do great things for God despite our past mistakes. All we have to do is accept His forgiveness and *arise and go*!

Armour Up: I Timothy 1:12-17

Arise, Go.

CHAPTER FOUR
SANCTIFY YOURSELVES

Text: Joshua 3

Finally, it is time to cross the Jordan. Joshua rose early (vs. 1). No delay. No hesitation. He led the children of Israel to the edge of Jordan, and they waited there for further instruction. Three days pass, and then the officers went throughout the camp and gave the people some very important instruction.

What did the Ark of the Covenant represent to the nation of Israel (Exodus 25:22)?

Reread the command given to the people in verses Joshua 3:3-4. Why was it important for them to follow the Ark of the Covenant?

The Ark represented God's presence with them. By following the Ark of the Covenant, the people were following God. If we are going to move forward in our spiritual walk with the LORD, we must look to Him for guidance. Just as the children of Israel had "not passed this way heretofore" (vs. 4), we don't know what

ategorizationy.

lies ahead. We must look unto Jesus (Hebrews 12:1-2) and follow Him.

Joshua gives the next instruction. He tells the people, "Sanctify yourselves: for to morrow the LORD will do wonders among you" (vs. 5).

In the Old Testament, the people were often instructed to sanctify themselves. It was an act of preparation to come before the LORD. They were to be cleansed, purified, and hallowed unto God. The priests, the altars, and the instruments used in the sacrificial system were to be dedicated unto God for their sacred use and purpose.

In Exodus 19, the LORD told Moses to sanctify the people with instructions for them to cleanse themselves and their clothes. Married couples were to abstain from sexual activity and focus their attention on fasting and prayer (Exodus 19:15, I Corinthians 7:1-6).

We also see that God sanctified the people (Leviticus 20:8). He set them apart from other nations and called them "a peculiar treasure unto me" (Exodus 19:5). As His chosen people, He called them to be holy, "Ye shall be holy: for I the LORD your God am holy" (Leviticus 19:2).

In this same way, we have been sanctified at the point of salvation. When we accept Christ as our Savior, we are cleansed by His shed blood and

WHEN WE ACCEPT CHRIST AS OUR SAVIOR, WE ARE CLEANSED BY HIS SHED BLOOD AND PUT ON HIS RIGHTEOUSNESS.

put on His righteousness (Hebrews 10:10-14). We are adopted into God's family and become joint heirs with Christ (Galatians 4:4-7), and we are called to be holy and set apart unto the LORD (I Peter 1:15-16).

Once we become a child of God, we begin a process of sanctification that changes us to become more like Christ (Berg, 1999). Berg goes on to explain that many describe this as "…the process whereby the Spirit of God takes the Word of God and changes us to become like the Son of God" (p. 9). Some would simply call this spiritual growth, a topic that you know I am quite passionate about if you've read *Pullin' Weeds, Plantin' Seeds*.

> Sanctification (Webster's 1828 dictionary) – the act of making holy; the act of God's grace by which the affections of men are purified or alienated from sin and the world, and exalted to a supreme love to God.
>
> Reread that definition and underline any words or phrases that stand out to you.

There is so much packed into that definition that I have gone back to it again and again since first reading it. Notice that it is an "act of God's grace" meaning that we cannot do this alone. It is a cooperative journey between God and us (Berg, 1999).

The next thing I notice is the "affections of men are purified and alienated from sin and the world, and exalted to a supreme love to God." Such strong words: affections, purified, alienated, exalted, supreme. Let's pause here and do a little word study.

Look up the following words in Webster's 1828 Dictionary and record the most fitting definitions.

Affection

Purify

Alienate

Estrange

Exalted

Supreme

What are some of your affections?

Do any of them compete with your love for the LORD? If so, which ones?

What are we to do with those affections?

Practically speaking, what could you do to keep those things at a distance or withdraw them from your life (i.e. removing apps from your phone, deleting accounts, making guidelines for entertainment, shopping, technology, use of time, etc.)?

The second part of Joshua's instruction explains why the people were to sanctify themselves. He said, "...for to morrow the LORD will do wonders among you" (vs. 5). The LORD wanted to show them something amazing! He was going to allow them to personally experience the parting of the Jordan river. After years of wandering in the wilderness, only Caleb, Joshua, and the "little ones" (Numbers 14:31) had seen the miraculous crossing of the Red Sea. Now the entire nation would see God's work firsthand.

As I studied this through, I couldn't help but wonder how many times I missed out on seeing God's wonders in my life because I was holding onto affections of this world. Is the LORD asking that we "sanctify" ourselves so He can freely work in our lives? I think so.

Remember I mentioned in the introduction that I had crossed over into the Victorious Christian Life. I realized that the LORD had more for me as I walked with Him on this earth. I no longer needed to "go through the motions" of Christianity. Instead, I could experience a personal relationship with the LORD that allowed me to see Him at work in my life each and every day.

I'd like to compare that decision to cross over into the Victorious Christian Life with surrendering to the process of sanctification. We have to be willing to submit to the Holy Spirit's leading in our lives and say, "Yes, LORD." We have to decide that we want more from our relationship with the LORD, and that more will take an ongoing self-examination of the affections that we allow to creep into our lives which compete with our supreme love for the LORD.

Imagine you are standing at the banks of the Jordan River. Your Captain, the Lord Jesus Christ, has given the instruction. Sanctify yourself. Let go of anything holding you back and prepare to *arise and go*. Tomorrow—and every day after—you will see wonders among you. Choose.

Armour Up: Psalm 119:9-16

Arise, Go.

CHAPTER FIVE
MOVING FORWARD

Text: Joshua 3-4

With the decision to cross over into the Victorious Christian Life made, the next step seems easy.

Move forward.

And keep moving forward.

As I mentioned in the introduction, the decision to cross over into the Victorious Christian Life was really only a small step on my journey with the Lord. Experiencing the Victorious Christian Life takes diligent, continual effort to maintain a right relationship with the Lord. It takes daily, consistent time with the Lord in His Word and in prayer. It takes being obedient to His Word and surrendering my will. And if we never want to "go back" to a dry, empty Christian life, it means we must keep moving forward with the Lord.

In the previous chapter, we briefly considered the Ark of the Covenant and its representation of the presence of God. The people were to follow the Ark of the Covenant as they moved forward to cross the Jordan River. The Jordan River at that time was overflowing its banks (vs. 15). It would have been a raging, rushing river that according to some may have been a mile wide.

We live near El Dorado Lake here in Kansas. When the lake gets too full, they open the spillway and water rushes into the Walnut River. The water races downstream with such force, it is frightening to think of anyone getting out on the water or attempting to cross it. Of course, the Walnut River is nowhere near a mile wide, but the visual gives me some idea of what the Jordan River would have been like at that time.

Imagine Joshua staring out over the raging, rushing water and considering how he could possibly lead the men, women, children, and supplies across to the other side. He probably thought back to when the Egyptian army had Moses and the previous generation up against the Red Sea. No doubt it gave him courage because we see no evidence of hesitation or attempting to delay for a more opportune time to cross the river. He knew God had parted the Red Sea and had faith that He would do the same thing as they faced the Jordan River.

The priests did not have that personal experience to embolden them. They had to obey Joshua's command to take up the Ark and step into the Jordan. It was only after the "feet of the priests that bare the ark were dipped in the brim of the water" (vs. 15) that God cut off the waters, and they stood firm on dry ground. The waters "failed, and were cut off" and "stood and rose up upon an heap" (vs. 16); and the people passed clean over Jordan on dry ground.

Imagine the sight! Consider the fear as they approached the overflowing Jordan river. Consider the faith it took to gather there and for the priests to step in.

God could have parted the Jordan long before the people approached the bank of the river. He wanted the people to be a part of the miracle—much like the disciples when He fed the 5,000 (Luke 9:10-17). He wanted them to exhibit faith and experience the wonder up close and personal.

According to Richard Hester, the crossing of the Jordan River brought the people to a crisis of faith. They were committing to struggle against the Canaan nations and to move forward with God without the possibility of retreat. He goes on to say, "…the Jordan crossing marked historically the time when the nation of Israel, weak, stubborn and sinful, came to the end of the defeated life of self, acknowledging their weakness, foolishness, and sinfulness. Conversely, they acknowledged by this act their willingness to trust alone in God for power, wisdom, guidance, and protection" (Hester, 2005).

The Promised Land did not promise a life of ease, free of conflict and suffering. The people had battles ahead of them, much like we do as we live out our time here on this earth. They needed to conquer and claim areas of the Promised Land, and we need to conquer areas of our spiritual lives as we claim more "ground" for the cause of Christ.

The crisis of faith for us is determining to "make the supreme choice of abandoning ourselves utterly to God's will, making Him first in our life...to bury all our self aims and desires in the swift waters of Jordan and pass on to that higher life where only the desires and purposes of our Lord are to be first" (Hester, 2005).

Let's take a closer look at our text (chapters 3 and 4) with the purpose of strengthening our faith. I think we'll find some helpful elements of faith that can apply to any crisis of faith we face— whether it is the initial "crossing over" or daily walking by faith.

Elements of Faith

1. Arise, go.

   Surprised to see our title here? As I attempted to find an antonym for the word hesitation, go was listed. It couldn't be more fitting. If we want to walk by faith, we must begin. We must step out without hesitation. Faith causes us to move forward with God even when we don't know the outcome.

   Record the phrases in the following verses that demonstrate the urgency or eagerness to follow God's will (3:1; 4:10):

2. Follow God.

    We do not know what the future holds for our lives; however, there is something incredibly comforting about remembering that nothing is a surprise to God. He knows what we will face each and every day, and He prepares us for it.

    Note Joshua's instructions regarding following the Ark (God) in 3:3-4. Consider the steps given: see, remove, go. How would those be applicable to stepping out by faith?

    What is significant about leaving "a space between you and it"?

3. God's Presence.

    While the Ark of the Covenant represented the presence of God for the Israelites, as believers we have the Holy Spirit of God indwelling us. We always have the presence of "the living God among us" (3:10).

    Read back through chapters 3 and 4 and note (underline, circle, highlight, etc.) each time the Ark is mentioned.
    How many times did you note?

    Why do you think this is significant?

How did Jesus describe the Holy Spirit in John 14:15-31? What words or phrases from this passage give you confidence and comfort in your ability to walk by faith?

4. Put Feet to It.

It was not until the feet of the priests were "dipped in the brim of the water" that the waters were stopped. The priests had to step out in faith. The people had to follow in faith, believing God would continue to hold the waters as they crossed the raging river.

UNLESS WE STEP OUT BY FAITH AND "GET OUR FEET WET," WE'RE NOT LIKELY TO MAKE MUCH PROGRESS IN LIVING FOR CHRIST AND SERVING HIM.

(Wiersbe, Be Strong, 1993)

Think of a time when the LORD called you to step out in faith. How did you have to "put feet to it"?

Take a moment to consider Proverb 3:5-6. What elements of faith do you see within this often quoted and familiar passage?

Examples of Faith

Let's take some time to explore a few examples of faith from Scripture. You may be familiar with the "Hall of Faith" found in Hebrews 11. Take some time to prayerfully read through this chapter and choose three examples to study. I've included an example in the table below to help you get started.

Examples of Faith		
Who did you choose?	**Where did you get more information?**	**What did you learn from his or her example?**
Gideon (vs. 32)	Judges 6-8	Gideon needed to obey by faith. He had to believe that God could use him – not because of who he was but because of Who God was (is)! Gideon and his army were not great warriors. They were willing and obedient. God is still looking to work through willing people today. Have faith and obey!

Examples of Faith (cont.)		
Who did you choose?	Where did you get more information?	What did you learn from his or her example?

Encouragement of Faith

As we wrap up this chapter, I want to take a moment to encourage you to move forward in faith. Encouragement is the act of giving courage, or confidence of success; incitement to action; to promote or *advance* (Webster's 1828 Dictionary – emphasis mine). We need to advance, to move forward in our walk with the LORD.

Practically speaking, what exactly does moving forward with the LORD look like? Well, it will be different for each of us because we are all in different stages of our Christian life. Some may need to step out in faith by being obedient in the basics – time in God's Word, prayer, church attendance, tithing on their income and faith promise giving. Others who are further along in their walk with the LORD may be asked to step out in faith in other ways.

We *all* must step out by faith and do what the LORD calls us to do. Too often I see people who are stuck in their walk with the LORD. They are always searching for the LORD's will and unwilling to act on what has already been revealed to them. They are hesitant to make decisions or changes in their lives because they fear making a mistake. I'll be the first to admit that I have made plenty of mistakes in my life; however, I can say with confidence that I have never made a mistake that the LORD did not use to grow me in my walk with Him and give me more knowledge and wisdom for when I would face a similar circumstance.

My husband, Marc, and I have gone through a lot of changes this past year. We sold the house in the country we had lived in for 15 years and moved to town. Marc left a comfortable job he had for 15 years for a better working environment with less pay. I began to pray about expanding my writing ministry and stationery business and what that would mean for my "day job."

None of these decisions were *easy* or *comfortable* for me. We diligently prayed over each of them and then took steps in the direction we believed the LORD was leading us. I can remember praying often, "If this is not your will, please shut—no slam—the door!" We knew these were big changes and absolutely did not want to do anything outside of the LORD's will. I can look back now and see how the LORD slowly prepared my heart for each change, led us along the way, and carefully orchestrated each and every step (more on that in the next chapter).

WE NEVER STAND STILL IN THE CHRISTIAN LIFE; WE EITHER MOVE FORWARD IN FAITH OR GO BACKWARD IN UNBELIEF.

(Wiersbe, Be Strong, 1993)

Warren Wiersbe said, "Christians are either overcome because of unbelief or overcomers because of their faith" (Wiersbe, Be Available, 1993). I don't know about you, but I want to be an overcomer. I want to have a faith that keeps me moving forward with the LORD. When we are faced with a crisis of faith, like the children of Israel at the brink of the

Jordan River, we must surrender our will, our plans, and our desires, and put our trust in God alone for a future that seems uncertain to us. Thankfully, the future is never uncertain for Him or with Him.

Armour Up: Psalm 37:23-24; Psalm 18:30-36

Arise, Go.

CHAPTER SIX
TAKE TIME TO REMEMBER

Text: Joshua 4

The LORD wanted the nation of Israel to have a memorial to remind them of His deliverance. He instructed Joshua to have twelve stones representing the twelve tribes removed from the midst of the Jordan and set up in Gilgal as a memorial. Interestingly, we see another memorial was set up in the midst of the Jordan (vs. 9).

Look up the following in Webster's 1828 dictionary and record the definitions here:

Remembrance -

Memorial (noun) –

In the last chapter, we discussed the nation of Israel was in a *crisis* of faith as they approached the crossing of the Jordan. The word crisis in this sense means "to determine, to decide; or a decisive state of things" (Webster's 1828). They had to make a decision to leave all that was comfortable and familiar and move forward with God, trusting Him alone for their safety and provision as they entered into the Promised Land.

"A faith which is victorious in its crisis leaves a memorial behind" (Hester, 2005). And in this case, the children of Israel left two memorials behind. Let's take a closer look.

What instruction did the LORD give Joshua concerning the memorial in vs. 1-3?

Where were they supposed to erect the memorial (vs. 3, 19-20)?

What was the memorial for (vs. 6-7, 21-24)?

What are we told about the other memorial (vs. 9)?

Who set up the twelve stones in the midst of the Jordan?

It's interesting to me that Joshua set up the twelve stones in the midst of the Jordan. There is no mention of the chosen men helping with this particular memorial. The memorial in the midst of the water represented Christ's judgment in our place (Scofield, 1917). As we learned in the first chapter, Joshua is a picture of Christ. Who better to erect that memorial than the man who was a picture of Christ? The buried stones would remind the nation of Israel that their old life was buried under the waters of the Jordan, and they would be entering into the Promised Land where they were to walk in a new life of obedience to the LORD.

The memorial that was set up in Gilgal represents the believer's deliverance (Scofield, 1917). It was to be a reminder to the nation of Israel of the miraculous crossing of the Jordan and the Red Sea (vs. 23). It signified the end of the wandering in the wilderness and their deliverance from Egypt. God wanted them to be able to tell future generations of the mighty power by which He delivered them from their enemies.

Crisis of Faith

We will all face what could be considered crises of faith in our Christian life. This doesn't necessarily mean we are doubting our salvation or a belief in God. It is simply a time when we believe the LORD is leading us in a certain direction, and we must make a decision. I mentioned in the previous chapter that we all must step out by faith and do what the LORD calls us to do. It could be what college we will attend, which job we will take (or leave), which church we should join, where we should live, or the ministry in which we should be involved. Once we make a decision, believing we are following the LORD's will, what do we do when it gets hard? Does that mean we were wrong?

Sometimes. That's comforting, isn't it? None of us are perfect. There will be times when we misread the LORD's direction or mistake our own desires with His guidance, but remember, those are opportunities for the LORD to grow us in our walk with Him and for us to gain knowledge and wisdom for the future.

Other times when things get hard, we are right where God wants us to be. Difficulty does not necessarily mean we are out of God's will. Jesus even tells the disciples, "...In the world ye shall have tribulation:" (John 16:33). However, our natural instinct when things aren't going as smoothly as we think they should be is to begin to doubt. We question God. We question our ability to discern His will in our lives. And we may even start looking for the first 'escape route.'

DIFFICULTY DOES NOT NECESSARILY MEAN WE ARE OUT OF GOD'S WILL.

It's in those times that we need a memorial to look back to which will remind us of His leading in our life. Without memorials set up along the way in our Christian life, we will begin to doubt.

In the last chapter, I told you of the many changes that had taken place in our lives this last year. It started a few years ago with Marc telling me he wanted to move back to town. My first response was an immediate, "No!" We had spent years DIYing that house to make it what we wanted it to be. I loved living in the country and had no desire to move back to town. As I began to pray about it, however, the LORD changed my heart—little by little.

We began a long search for a new home. With Chaz and Harley out of the house, we thought it was time to downsize. As I looked at each house, it was as if the Lord asked me if I was willing to surrender "my stuff" – the farmhouse table we had custom made, furniture we had built with the kids, the quiet, country living I so enjoyed. Would I be willing to give up all of those "comforts"?

It was a slow process. The housing market was hot and decisions had to be made quickly. Content in our current home, we were in no rush to move. We even stopped looking for a time, believing the LORD was telling us to wait.

One Wednesday after church on the long drive home, I happened to see a house in my email from the housing website we had been using. I knew right away that this was our house, so much so that I was scared to go look at it. It was in May, one of the busiest times of year for me. I was getting ready for a relaxing summer break, and I knew buying a house and moving was anything but relaxing. Chaz was graduating from Heartland the following week, and we had plans to spend the week in Oklahoma City. We ended up putting an offer on the house which was accepted, rushing to get our house listed to sell, and leaving everything in our realtor's hands as we headed out of town.

The thought of all these pieces needing to fall together made me a little anxious. I remember getting up one night and reading over God's promises from His Word and recalling all the times— the memorials—the LORD had taken care of us over the years. We may have had some difficult financial times in the past, but He had always provided for us and worked all things out for our good.

Over the next weeks, God's perfect plan and timing was revealed over and over again. My father-in-law unexpectedly went home to be with the LORD. Our new house would only be five blocks from my mother-in-law's house. We sold our country home quickly and for more than we had hoped. The timing of moving out and moving in worked out so smoothly. We truly had confirmation every step of the way that we were making the move at the perfect time.

It was important for us to have those memorials as we moved in and started to experience some of the pains of owning a new home. New heating and air conditioning. A bathroom remodel that didn't go as planned. A broken main water line. We could have easily become frustrated and questioned if we had done the right thing, but instead we could look back and be reminded of God's hand of provision and direction through the entire process.

Another example of memorials that have been important in the lives of our children has been when they surrendered to the ministry. They each had periods of difficulty during their time at

Bible college and preparation for ministry. They have had to take time to remember when God first put it on their heart to surrender to whatever He asked them to do. Those memorials have encouraged them to keep pressing on in their journey with the LORD.

Hopefully, you are already thinking of some memorials set up in your past that you are able to look to for confirmation of the LORD's leading in your life. Take a few minutes to record some of those now.

Start at the beginning of your walk with the LORD. If we have accepted Christ as our Savior, we all have a Salvation Memorial (testimony of when and where you accepted Christ as your Savior):

What other memorials can you think of that have been significant in your life?

Purpose of Memorials

God wanted to give the nation of Israel a memorial to remember His power, strength, presence, and deliverance. However, it was not just for the benefit of their own personal faith and walk with the LORD. The memorials were to be a sign to the next generation (vs. 6-7) and to all the people of the earth (vs. 24). When we walk with the LORD, our faith will be seen by others. We can be a living memorial to those around us of God's goodness, mercy, and grace.

The Bible is filled with examples of God instructing people to build an altar or a memorial as a sign of remembrance. He knew the importance of teaching the next generation and the consequences when His people failed to do so. They would forget the LORD and all He had done for them. Of course, we know that is exactly what happened (Judges 2:10; Psalm 78; Psalm 106).

Israel's failure in this area does not alleviate our responsibility to teach our children the ways of the LORD. We have been given the complete Word of God and the indwelling of the Holy Spirit. If anything, the downward spiral of the nation of Israel thoroughly recorded in the book of Judges should motivate us to be more diligent in teaching and training our children.

Read Deuteronomy 6:1-9. I realize that not all who are reading this will have children in their home, but I believe each of us can influence the children in our lives for the LORD (grandparents, aunts, teachers, children's ministry workers, faithful church members, etc.).

Who has the primary responsibility to teach children the Word of God?

What three things should be evident in the lives of parents if we are going to successfully teach our children (vs. 2, 6)?

What should be our motivation for living for the LORD and teaching and training our children (vs. 3-5)?

When and how should we be teaching our children?

This passage lays out the responsibility parents have to teach our children the Word of God—purposefully within the daily rhythms of life. It is not something that can be confined to a church building or the Sunday School teacher. Parents (and other influential adults) must "teach them diligently" (Deuteronomy 6:7) by taking every opportunity to point their children to God and the Truth of His Word. Not only should we talk about the memorials we have in our past as evidence of God's working in our lives, but we should also be living memorials, demonstrating the fear of the LORD, knowledge of His Word, and obedience to It.

As we bring this chapter to a close, remember the importance of the memorials the Israelites set up in the midst of the Jordan and in Gilgal did not stop with teaching the next generation. Joshua 4:24 says, "That all the people of the earth might know the hand of the LORD, that it is mighty: that ye might fear the LORD your God for ever."

God shows Himself mighty in our lives for the strengthening of our faith and as a testimony to the world. Are you living in such a way that shows you know the LORD? Is your life a reminder to those around you that He is the LORD your God?

Armour Up: 2 Peter 1:12-21

Arise, Go.

CHAPTER SEVEN
THE CUTTING AWAY

Text: Joshua 5

With the crossing of the Jordan River behind them, the Israelites were no longer wandering. They were back in fellowship with God and needed to follow through in some important areas of obedience. The battles they would soon face in their efforts to conquer the Promised Land required a time of spiritual preparation. It started with circumcision.

What did circumcision signify (Genesis 17:9-14, 23-27)?

Why was it necessary to "circumcise again" the children of Israel "the second time" (Joshua 5:2-7)?

How did the LORD ensure their safety as they followed through with this step of obedience (Joshua 5:1, 8)?

Circumcision was a sign of the covenant God had made with Abraham. It was to be an outward symbol to remind them that their bodies belonged to the LORD, and they were to live a life set apart to God. The act of circumcision had been put on hold after the people refused to believe God and enter into the Promised Land. It was important for the new generation to renew their covenant relationship with the LORD so they would be prepared for the temptations that awaited them in a land filled with pagan people (Wiersbe, Be Strong, 1993).

While circumcision was required of the nation of Israel, God has always been interested in more than an outward show of His relationship with them. God wanted it to reflect a "circumcision of the heart" (Deut. 10:12-16; 30:16) which produced a love for Him that motivated them to obey His commandments and serve Him.

Following the circumcision, the LORD said, "This day have I rolled away the reproach of Egypt from off you" (vs. 9). A reproach is something that causes shame or disgrace. The Israelites were not in sin for being in Egypt. God had orchestrated the events that led them there; however, over time they had been enslaved and His attempt to free them and bring them into the Promised Land had been postponed by their unbelief. It was this sin and the wandering in the wilderness that brought shame to the nation of Israel. Now they were in the Promised Land and that reproach was "rolled away."

The circumcision also qualified them to participate in the Passover again (Exodus 12:43-48), the next important step of obedience we see in chapter five. God wanted the Jews to remember their bondage in Egypt and how He had delivered them so He instituted the Passover as a Memorial.

THEY WERE NEVER TO FORGET THAT THEY WERE A REDEEMED PEOPLE, SET FREE BY THE BLOOD OF THE LAMB.

(Wiersbe, Be Strong, 1993)

Take some time to read about the Passover in Exodus 12:1-13:10 and answer the following questions:

When was the Passover to be celebrated (Exodus 12:2-6; 13:4)? Look up Abib in Webster's 1828 dictionary for more information.

When did the people enter Canaan (Joshua 4:19)? What does that tell you about God?

Why was this Memorial instituted (Exodus 12:14, 24-27; 13:3-10)?

What similarities do you notice in the Passover lamb and Jesus Christ?

Christ Our Passover
Dig deeper.
What can you learn about Christ our Passover?

John 1:29, 36

I Corinthians 5:6-8

I Peter 1:17-21

Hebrews 4:14-16; 9:12-14; 10:10-12

Matthew 26:17-19; Mark 14:12-16; Luke 22:7-13

After celebrating the Passover, we see that "the manna ceased" (Joshua 5:12). The forty-year miracle of God's provision stopped because it was no longer needed. They were now in the Promised Land and able to eat of the fruit of the land of Canaan. According to Richard Hester, both the manna and the crops and fruits of Canaan typify Christ. He says, "He will not be to us as the rich crops and fruits of Canaan until after we have crossed the Jordan and come into the place of complete separation to Himself" (Hester, 2005).

Cutting Away

When I finally crossed over into the Victorious Christian Life, fully surrendered to the LORD and pursuing a personal relationship with Him, I quickly realized there was a need to circumcise—or cut away some things from my old life. You may remember that I was already attending church and my life was free of many of the "outward" sins that we like to focus on (Jesus actually has some harsh words about this in Matthew 23:23-28), but it was the inside that needed the most work. It was truly a "circumcision of the heart," and the process was slow and a bit painful.

I can remember that as I would draw closer to the LORD, He would reveal something to me that was not pleasing to Him. Maybe it was the tone of my voice. As I surrendered that to Him and began to work on it, another thing that needed to be cut away would be revealed. My tone reflected how easily I got frustrated or angry. Those would need attention too. Becoming frustrated and angry showed a lack of love and longsuffering. Examining my heart and seeking the LORD about these things always seemed to lead back to one issue—pride.

Being raised in a Christian home and attempting to live like a Christian made me think I was doing okay. It was easy to come out on top when I was comparing myself to others. It wasn't until I allowed God to use His measuring stick – the Word of God – that I could accurately and honestly see how much sin was hiding deep within my heart.

Let's take a few minutes to see what the Bible has to say about the circumcision of the heart. Look up the following passages and jot some notes about what you find.

Deuteronomy 10:12-16

Deuteronomy 30:6

Romans 2:17-29

Colossians 2:6-15

The cutting away that needs to take place in our life is a matter of putting away the flesh, the old man. We are to be "renewed in the spirit of your mind" and "put on the new man" (Ephesians 4:17-24). We are to be separated from this world through Christ and dedicated to living for the LORD each and every day.

I think we see the answer of how this is accomplished in our hearts and lives in Deuteronomy 10:12-13:

And now, Israel, what doth the LORD thy God require of thee, but to fear the LORD thy God, to walk in all his ways, and to love him, and to serve the LORD thy God with all thy heart and with all thy soul, To keep the commandments of the LORD, and his statutes, which I command thee this day for thy good?

Underline the verbs (action words) the LORD requires of us in the passage above.
Which ways are we to walk in?

How are we to do these things?

What does it mean to "fear the LORD" (see Webster's 1828 dictionary)?

Why did the LORD give us His commandments (Word)?

When we have a proper respect for the LORD and His authority in our lives, accompanied by an undivided love, we will desire to walk in His ways and keep His commandments. We will not be "stiffnecked" (Deuteronomy 10:16), choosing instead to submit to the process of cutting away the old man and putting on the new man. Deuteronomy 30:6 says, "…the LORD thy God will circumcise thine heart…" He is the one that does the cutting away; we just have to surrender to it and let Him work in our lives.

> WHEN WE HAVE A PROPER RESPECT FOR THE LORD AND HIS AUTHORITY IN OUR LIVES, ACCOMPANIED BY AN UNDIVIDED LOVE, WE WILL DESIRE TO WALK IN HIS WAYS AND KEEP HIS COMMANDMENTS.

One final note from our text that is significant here. It was only after Israel had been obedient in the circumcision and observing the Passover, that we see the LORD appear to Joshua to give him direction for their next steps (5:13-15). The "captain of the host of the LORD" is none other than the Captain of our Salvation that we discussed in chapter one. This was a preincarnation appearance of the Lord Jesus Christ. His appearance would have been reassurance for Joshua that he was not alone, but also to remind him of his place in leading the people. Joshua was second in command and would need to remember that as they began their conquest of the land. We see Joshua willing to submit and ready to hear the battle plan for taking Jericho (6:2-5).

When we are submitted to walking in obedience to the LORD and His Word, we will be better able to recognize His presence and His leading in our lives. We will have confidence that we are not alone as we face spiritual battles in our daily Christian life. We can continue moving forward with God in victory!

As you work on your "Armour Up" for this chapter, ask yourself what is in need of cutting away?

Armour Up: Colossians 3:1-17

Arise, Go.

CHAPTER EIGHT
VICTORY AND DEFEAT

Text: Joshua 6-8

As we dig into these three chapters, remember to consider the victories and defeat the nation of Israel faced in parallel to the spiritual battles we face living the Victorious Christian Life. As we attempt to walk with the LORD, we will have "mountain top experiences" (victories) and times in the "valley" (defeats). We must remain faithful through the victories and defeats we experience, drawing ever closer to the LORD.

Our text opens with Joshua receiving the marching orders (quite literally) from the LORD to conquer Jericho. I'm sure to him it was an unexpected and interesting battle plan. The people were to march around the city once each day for six days. On the seventh day, they would march around the city seven times, followed by the priests blowing the trumpets. When the people heard the trumpets, they were to shout with a great shout. The LORD assured Joshua that the walls surrounding Jericho would fall down flat, and they would be able to take the city.

What was Joshua's response to the LORD's battle plan (vs. 6-7, 12)?

When the LORD gives you direction, are you quick to obey? Or do you question and hesitate to surrender?

There was wisdom in Joshua's instruction to the people to keep quiet (6:10). He tells them, "Ye shall not shout, nor make any noise with your voice, neither shall any word proceed out of your mouth…" This instruction left no opportunity for murmuring—something the people had a history of doing when they couldn't see God's plan.

Do you tend to murmur and complain rather than trust?

What does the LORD have to say about murmuring and complaining (See Exodus 16:8; Philippians 2:14-16)?

NO WALL IS TOO HIGH, NO BARRIER SO IMPENETRABLE, AND NO SIN SO GREAT THAT OUR LORD JESUS CHRIST CANNOT GIVE US THE VICTORY.

(Trotter, 2019)

Now let's talk about the great shout and the victory that followed. When the priests blew the trumpets, the people were to shout with a great shout. Why? God had already given them the victory (6:16). It was to be a shout of praise!

They were to "Reckon on God's promise. Count it as well as done, giving glory to God" (Hester, 2005).

As the people shouted, the walls of Jericho fell down flat just as God promised. The people went up into the city and utterly destroyed it. Only Rahab and her family were saved. Sometimes when we read these accounts in the Bible, we can question why God would destroy these people. We must understand that these nations were evil and had refused to turn to the LORD. He used the nation of Israel to execute judgment on them. God is the Righteous Judge. It is a characteristic that we in today's society don't like to consider, but there is coming a day when Jesus Christ will return and judge the earth in righteousness (Revelation. 19).

The LORD *gave* them the city. Once again, we see our All-Powerful God allowed them to be a part of something miraculous. He did not need them to march around the city, but He wanted them to experience the victory. As a result, "So the LORD was with Joshua; and his fame was noised throughout all the country" (6:27). When we are walking in victory with the LORD, people will take notice. They will see something different in us, and it will open doors of opportunity to be a witness to others.

From Great Victory to Embarrassing Defeat

Joshua and the people, emboldened by the conquest of Jericho, set their sights on Ai. They confidently say, "Let not all the people go up...for they are but few" (7:3). Joshua failed to consult God for the battle plan, thirty-six men died, and "the hearts of the people melted" (7:5). How quickly things had changed!

It's easy for us to look at the account of Ai and see the people were overconfident and failed to consult God. We are all guilty of the same thing. Remember those mountaintop experiences I mentioned at

WE ARE NOT ABLE TO FIGHT EVEN THE SMALLEST ATTACKS OF SATAN APART FROM GOD.

(Hester, 2005)

the beginning of this chapter? When things are going well, we tend to plunge ahead in our own strength, our own wisdom. We approach our daily life as "small attacks" which can be handled without relying on God. We would never *say* it, but our attitude and actions show we don't need God. However, it is after great spiritual victories that we need to be the most on guard. The enemy knows our tendency to let our guard down and rely on our own strength, and he will be ready to pounce (I Peter 5:8).

Joshua's response to the defeat is to immediately fall on his face before the LORD. His posture was correct. His words, however, were a bit accusatory and a little too similar to the murmurings and complaints of the people when they had wandered in the wilderness (7:7; Exodus 16:3, 17:3). The LORD responds, "Get thee up; wherefore liest thou thus upon thy face?" (7:10). When things go wrong, we would be wise to take some time to look inward before blaming and questioning God.

Sin in the Camp

"But the children of Israel committed a trespass in the accursed thing:" (7:1). This explained everything.

Reread Joshua 6:18-19. What were the instructions and consequences given regarding the plunder of Jericho?

Achan's story gives us a perfect example of the progression of sin and the devastating consequences that follow. He saw the items. He coveted them. He took them. He hid them.

Achan knew he wasn't supposed to take the items. The instruction had been very clear. But somewhere during what was probably only a few moments, he somehow excused disobeying God's Word and acted upon it. Then he attempted to hide it, thinking no one would ever know. He probably even thought he had gotten away with it as there were no immediate consequences for his actions.

But the consequences did come. For the nation of Israel as they faced an embarrassing defeat at the hands of Ai. And for Achan and his family.

Achan's sin affected them all—corporately. It reached beyond his family and friends and caused judgment on the entire nation. We cannot ignore the similarities that take place when there is unconfessed sin in our local churches. It affects the whole body of believers. God takes sin seriously. We are guilty of hiding it, denying it, and minimizing it. However, secret sin will be found out one way or another. Eventually "sin's roll call" (7:13-26) will take place (Gaddis, 2018).

I often wonder what would have happened if Achan would have immediately repented. Or maybe after the defeat at Ai. Or maybe after the warning of judgment coming the next morning. Throughout the Bible, we see God willing to extend mercy. Perhaps the punishment would have been less severe. Maybe his family could have been spared.

The truth is that if we were taking "sin's roll call" as Bro. Gaddis calls it, we would all be guilty. He goes on in that message to explain that there is not one of us who are sinless. But if we are living the Victorious Christian Life, we should be sinning less. There will still be times when we sin as we discussed back in chapter three. It is our response to our sin that matters.

Arise. Go. Do.

After "the LORD turned from the fierceness of his anger" (7:26), He immediately reassures Joshua with a familiar charge. "Fear not, neither be thou dismayed" (8:1). Aren't you thankful the LORD is willing to reassure us over and over again?

Look up the following verses and be encouraged! What does God promise?

Deuteronomy 31:6-8

Deuteronomy 31:23

Joshua 1:5-9

Isaiah 41:10

Psalm 34:4

II Timothy 1:7

The LORD reminds Joshua not to be afraid and commands him to take action. Arise, go. The sin had been dealt with and God was once again with them. It was time to get back to work. Arise, go, *do*. The same is true for us. We've already discussed how we cannot let our past failures hold us back. Instead, we must keep pressing forward in our walk with Him.

Joshua lays out the battle plan, using their past retreat as a tactic for victory. He reassures the people, "...the LORD your God will deliver it [Ai] into your hand" (8:7). Once again, we see Joshua rise up early (8:10) and get the people organized for the attack. The battle unfolds just as God said, and Israel once again experiences a great victory.

After they take Ai and divide the spoil (8:2, 27), Joshua pauses the military campaign to build an altar (Joshua 8:30-35; Deuteronomy 27). The priests offered burnt offerings and sacrificed peace offerings to the LORD. It was a sign of their commitment to God and expressing their thanksgiving for His faithful care of them. Joshua was drawing the attention of the people to the LORD. Only He deserved the honor and glory for the victories over Jericho and Ai.

Finally, Joshua read the law to the people. He reiterates the blessings and cursings from the law as Moses had instructed him to do (Deuteronomy 27). It would be up to the people to choose to continue following the LORD or to turn away from Him. It's a choice we all face each and every day.

As we continue our journey with the LORD walking in the Victorious Christian Life, we will have great victories. We must remember in those times to give all the glory to God while also being on guard for Satan's next attack. But our journey will also include defeats. Not all of our defeats will be the result of sin, but we must be careful to have a tender heart toward the LORD. David invited the LORD to examine his heart (Psalm 26:2; 139: 23-24) to ensure there was no sin in his life. We won't be able to stand against the attacks of Satan if we have sin in our lives. We must always be ready to pray as David did, "Create in me a clean heart, O God; and renew a right spirit within me" (Psalm 51:10).

Armour Up: Romans 6

Arise, Go.

CHAPTER NINE
BEWARE OF SATAN'S
ATTACKS

Text: Joshua 9-10

As the kings of the land began to rally together to fight against the Israelites, we see one particular group stand out and apart from all the rest – the Gibeonites. The Gibeonites were sneaky and deceptive and represent the wiles of the devil in our spiritual battles.

What word is used to describe how the Gibeonites worked (vs. 4-5)? Use Webster's 1828 dictionary or Strong's concordance to gain a better understanding of wilily.

How did the Gibeonites deceive Joshua and the men of Israel (vs. 4-13)?

Why did Joshua and the men of Israel fall for the deception (9:14)? And what was the result (9:15)?

Look up the following in Webster's 1828 dictionary and record the definitions here:

League -

What had God said about making leagues?
Exodus 23:31-33; 34:12; Numbers 33:55; Deuteronomy 7:1-2

It is worth noting that once again after a victory, we see Joshua and the men of Israel make a serious mistake. They failed to seek counsel of the LORD—just as they had when planning their first attempt to defeat Ai. If these men of God were susceptible to relying on their own strength and wisdom so soon after their experience with Ai, we can be certain that the same is true for us. We must always seek counsel of the LORD regardless of how much we trust someone or how "right" something seems.

The Israelites formed a league with the Gibeonites, only to find out they had been deceived. They had sworn in the name of the LORD and could not go back on their oath. Their solution was to turn the Gibeonites into bondservants responsible for hauling water and fuel for the service of the tabernacle.

While the league was not according to God's plan, we do see that He is able to use even our mistakes to accomplish His purpose. The Gibeonites call on Joshua and the Israelites for protection (Joshua 10:1-6), and this leads to more conquests for the Israelites (more on this in the next chapter).

Satan's Tactics

When you think of Satan's tactics, what are some things that come to mind?

The best picture of Satan and how he uses his tactics against us can be found in the beginning. In the account in Genesis 3:1-6, we see Satan disguise himself as a serpent. He makes his temptations look pleasing to us, appealing to us. Let me mention here that what appeals to one person may not appeal to another, so Satan will be careful to personalize the temptations he puts before us.

> SATAN'S SUBTLE WILES ARE MORE DANGEROUS THAN HIS OPEN ASSAULTS.
>
> (Baxter, 1976)

91

Not only will Satan disguise himself (II Corinthians 11:14) and his temptations, but he is also the great deceiver. He is a liar, and the father of it (John 8:44). This is his primary tactic. His lies will cause us to question God's Word, His character, and His promises.

Look up the following verses. What do you notice about the enemy?

Ephesians 6:11, 16

I Peter 5:8; Job 1:6-7

John 8:44; Revelation 12:9

Ephesians 2:1-2; II Corinthians 4:4; I John 5:19

Satan hates God, His Word, and His people. He will do everything he can to steal, kill, and destroy (John 10:10). He is actively working to ensure that those who are lost and do not know God stay that way (Matthew 13:19; II Corinthians 4:3-4). At the same time, he is attempting to destroy the lives of those who are saved and thus ruin any opportunity they have to win others to Christ.

Fight Back

We've already seen from our text the importance of taking everything to God in prayer. The big things. The seemingly small things. As I've studied for this Bible study the last few years, I have been more mindful to pray every morning and ask the LORD to prepare me for what lies ahead, help me to discern attacks from the enemy (or even my own flesh), and be ready to stand in faith. The LORD knows what each day will bring for me, and it gives me great peace to leave the day in His capable hands. Prayer truly is our first line of defense against Satan's "fiery darts" (Ephesians 6:18).

What fiery darts are most dangerous for you? Remember Satan will disguise and personalize his temptations just for you.

As we discussed briefly in chapter two, our offensive weapon against Satan's attacks is the Word of God. Jesus skillfully used God's Word against Satan when He was tempted in the wilderness.

What can you learn from Jesus's example in Matthew 4:1-11?

We must know God's Word. Jesus was able to quote Scripture in response to Satan's attacks. Do we know the Bible that well? Do we spend time reading It, studying It, and meditating upon It? Is God's Word hidden within our hearts (Psalm 119:11)? Our knowledge of God's Word allows us to exercise godly wisdom, and wisdom is directly connected to our ability to discern and recognize Satan's sneaky attacks against us.

Read Proverbs 2, define the terms using Webster's 1828 dictionary, and answer the following questions:

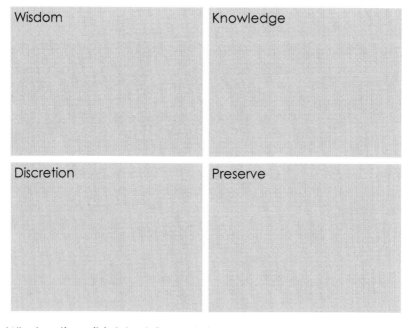

Wisdom	Knowledge
Discretion	Preserve

What actions (hint: look for verbs) do we take to obtain wisdom (vs. 1-4)?

Then what happens (vs. 6-9)?

"When wisdom entereth into thine heart, and knowledge is pleasant unto thy soul; Discretion shall preserve thee, understanding shall keep thee: To deliver thee…" (vs. 10-12a). Practicing discernment delivers us from evil influences and allows us to recognize attacks which threaten to turn our hearts from the LORD and destroy our fellowship with Him. We must exercise wisdom "That thou mayest walk in the way of good men, and keep the paths of the righteous" (vs. 20).

Armour Up: I Corinthians 10:12-13

Arise, Go.

CHAPTER TEN
THE LORD WILL FIGHT
FOR YOU

Text: Joshua 10-14

The LORD fought for Israel (10:14, 42)! This phrase should bring us so much excitement and encouragement. The LORD fought for Israel and continues to fight for His people today! We have spent several chapters of this study

We will be reading more chapters from our text as our study comes to a close. While we will not cover all of the events recorded in these final chapters, I do want you to have the full context as we move forward.

digging into our part in the spiritual battle. Now we are going to focus on the LORD and His promises to help us on our journey in the Victorious Christian Life.

Read back through chapters 10-11. This time, take note of any words or phrases that reveal how the LORD fought for Israel:

Imagine as Joshua looked out over the forces that had joined together to fight them. They were described "...as the sand that is upon the sea shore in multitude" (11:4), but the LORD lovingly reassures Joshua again. "Be not afraid because of them: for to morrow about this time will I deliver them up..." (11:6).

THESE THINGS I HAVE SPOKEN UNTO YOU, THAT IN ME YE MIGHT HAVE PEACE. IN THE WORLD YE SHALL HAVE TRIBULATION: BUT BE OF GOOD CHEER; I HAVE OVERCOME THE WORLD.

John 16:33

We are not alone in our battles! As we live our life here on earth, we will face spiritual battles with the enemy. But we will also have times of trials and tribulation that are simply the result of living in a fallen world. Jesus promised tribulation would come in John 16:33, "...In the world ye shall have tribulation..." However, in that same verse He reassures us and encourages us with His peace and His victory over this world.

Use the Strong's Concordance to define the word tribulation in John 16:33:

Like Joshua, we will have times when the trouble we are facing seems too great and threatens to overwhelm us, but God is faithful to remind us that we are not alone. He wants to fight for us!

98

The LORD Delivers

"Fear them not: for I have delivered them into thine hand;" (10:8).

"…the LORD your God hath delivered them into your hand" (10:19).

"And the LORD delivered it also…" (10:30)

"And the LORD delivered…" (10:32)

"Be not afraid because of them: for to morrow about this time will I deliver them up…" (11:6)

"And the LORD delivered them into the hand of Israel…" (11:8).

The LORD delivered their enemies into the hand of Israel. The applicable definition of the word deliver here means to give, or transfer; to put into another's hand or power (Webster's 1828). The LORD gave them victory over their enemies. He gave them the cities. He gave them the land.

While the LORD will deliver our enemies into our hands, He is also our Deliverer. He has promised to deliver—to free, release, rescue, and to save—us in the midst of our times of tribulation. We want immediate deliverance when in the midst of a trying time, but the meaning of deliver can include to *carry through*. Sometimes instead of an immediate rescue, we must patiently endure the trial while trusting the LORD will carry us through to the other side.

Arise, Go.

Take some time to look up the following verses, take a few notes and be encouraged. The LORD delivers!

Psalm 25:20

Psalm 34:4

Psalm 34:17, 19

Psalm 37:40

Psalm 50:15

Psalm 54:7

The LORD Defends

As the children of Israel went into battle after battle, they had to trust the LORD to defend them, to protect them from harm. The same is true for us. We can put on the armour of God and prepare for battle (see chapter two), but the LORD is our defense (Psalm 59:9, 16-17). He is our refuge and strength (Psalm 46:1), our help and our shield (Psalm 33:20).

Look up the following words related to how the LORD defends in the Webster's 1828 dictionary:

Defend

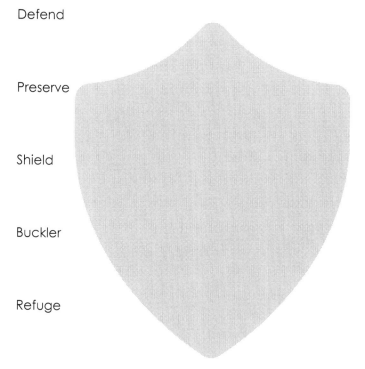

Preserve

Shield

Buckler

Refuge

Now use a Bible concordance to choose a favorite verse(s) for each of the words (or a form of them – i.e. defence for defend) above. Meditate on them and commit them to memory.

A few years ago, I was becoming increasingly discouraged by the direction our country was headed. I felt under attack as I attempted to stand for what was right, to be set apart, and not accept or tolerate the moral decline of our society. It seemed like I needed to *defend* my stance on Biblical truth, and I knew that I would fall short when trying to articulate my position.

The LORD encouraged me with Psalm 5:11-12, "But let all those that put their trust in thee rejoice: let them ever shout for joy, because thou defendest them: let them also that love thy name be joyful in thee. For thou, LORD, wilt bless the righteous; with favour wilt thou compass him as with a shield."

I did not need to worry about defending myself because God would defend me. I could lovingly state my opinion, keep my reasons brief and based on Scripture, and leave the rest up to the LORD.

No matter what attacks we are facing in our Christian life, we can rest knowing the LORD defends us. When we put our trust in Him, and rely on His strength for the battle, we will have incredible peace and joy just as His Word promises.

Get in the Battle!

Joshua demonstrated great faith and obedience without wavering as they battled their enemies. He prayed bold prayers (10:12-14), made and implemented strategic battle plans (11:6-7), and left nothing undone that the LORD commanded (11:15). Joshua was *in* the battle.

As I studied these chapters, *"Get in the battle!"* kept running through my mind. It is written all over my notes and was a strong consideration for the title of this book. You may be thinking, I thought this chapter was about how the LORD will fight for us. And it is, but the LORD cannot fight for us if we aren't even in the battle.

Do we want to see God fight for us? Do we want to see Him work on our behalf? We must get in the battle.

We must keep moving forward in our Christian life. Don't be satisfied, settled. Instead, we continue to step out by faith and obediently conquer more ground for the LORD. We pray bold prayers, cry out to the LORD for His deliverance and defense. We get in the battle and let God fight for us.

Armour Up: II Kings 6:8-17

Arise, Go.

CHAPTER ELEVEN
POSSESS THE LAND

Text: Joshua 15-21

Before we draw from our text in this chapter, we need to back up for a moment and take a closer look at the inheritance the nation of Israel had been given. Their earthly inheritance was first promised to Abraham, called Abram at the time (Genesis 15:18-21). God promised him an everlasting possession in Genesis 17:8. He said, "And I will give unto thee, and to thy seed after thee, the land wherein thou art a stranger, all the land of Canaan, for an everlasting possession; and I will be their God."

We have read and studied how the nation of Israel finally entered The Promised Land centuries later and "made war a long time" (Joshua 11:18). It is estimated that it took five to seven years for the Israelites to conquer the land. It took diligent, persistent effort and endurance—much like our Christian lives and the spiritual battles we face.

Joshua 11:23 says, "So Joshua took the whole land, according to all that the LORD said unto Moses; and Joshua gave it for an inheritance unto Israel according to their divisions by their tribes. And the land rested from war."

This verse makes it seem the work was done. The inheritance had been given to Israel just as God commanded. After years of waiting, they had received their inheritance and could now enjoy dwelling in the Promised Land.

But wait...

At the beginning of chapter 13, we read, "Now Joshua was old and stricken in years; and the LORD said unto him, Thou art old and stricken in years, and there remaineth yet very much land to be possessed."

It is these two contrasting thoughts—the inheritance being given and very much land remaining to be possessed—that require us to dig deeper.

Inheritance vs. Possession

Bro. Richard Hester explains that the "decisive blow had been struck" in the conquering of the land (Hester, 2005). The key cities had been won; and enemy alliances crushed. Any remaining foes could be fought by individual tribes as they pressed on to possess the land.

Hester goes on to say, "So it is with us. The decisive blow has been struck at sin and Satan and the powers of darkness by our heavenly Captain; and thereby the entire inheritance of 'all blessings in the heavenlies in Christ' is ours; but we must now apply that victory, carrying it through the whole realm of our thought and life."

The inheritance was the whole land given by God. Our inheritance in Christ is what He is to us *potentially*. The possession was only the part claimed by faith. Our possession in Christ is what He is to us *practically* according to our faith (Hester, 2005).

Warren Wiersbe explains it this way, "Their ownership of the land was purely the gracious act of God, but their possession and enjoyment of the land depended on their submission and obedience to the Lord" (Wiersbe, Be Strong, 1993).

What eternal inheritance have we been given (Romans 8:16-17; Hebrews 9:15; I Peter 1:4)?

What earnest—a promise of what is to come—have we been given while we wait for our inheritance (Ephesians 1:13-14)?

We look forward to the day when we are given our eternal inheritance, but the LORD wants us to experience spiritual blessings now. He has left us His Word filled with exceeding great and precious promises (II Peter 1:4). Those promises are backed by the absolute integrity of God Himself and by all the power of His throne! Can you imagine?

Read II Peter 1:1-11.

What have we been given (vs. 3-4)?

What things should be in us—and abound (vs. 5-7)?

Why (vs. 8)?

There is a promise for our every need! He will never leave us or forsake us. His grace is sufficient. His compassions fail not. We can walk in the power of His might. Such wonderful promises— and so many more can be found in His Word. God keeps His promises. We have evidence of that all throughout the Bible.

The LORD has given us everything we need to be partakers of the divine nature – that is to be the new man, to walk in the Spirit. We have escaped the corruption. We can flee away from it now— not in our own strength. But by His strength. His power. He has given us everything we need to live a life pleasing to Him.

We are given these great and precious promises so we can live a life that will bring Him glory and draw others to Christ. That is our purpose on this earth. He doesn't give us those promises just so we will have a wonderful life. Our purpose is to see other people come to know Jesus as their Savior.

Think of all those promises found in God's Word as our earthly inheritance designed to help us live the Victorious Christian Life. This is what the LORD is to us *potentially*. The possession, for us then, is when we take hold of those promises and claim them for ourselves. We don't just believe them "in general" or "for others." We trust Him to fulfill those promises in our lives–no matter our current situation, no matter our circumstances, no matter the trials we face. We claim those promises by faith and take possession of them!

Slack Not

"And Joshua said unto the children of Israel, How long are ye slack to go to possess the land…?" (18:3).

What is the definition of slack?

What are some possible reasons the Israelites may have been slack to possess the land?

The Bible doesn't tell us why they were not eager to take possession of the land, but could it be that they were comfortable? That possessing meant work?

Each tribe was supposed to finish driving out the inhabitants of the inheritance they were given. They were to take up these battles themselves without relying on Joshua or the other tribes. Take the tribe of Joseph for example (17:14-18). They wanted more land, but they didn't want to work for it.

Once they possessed and settled into the land, they would need to work for their food, maintain their homes, make their clothes, etc. God had miraculously cared for their every need in the wilderness, and now there was work to do.

We have to do some work to possess all the LORD has for us as well. We should always desire *more* with God. It takes effort, obedience, commitment, and discipline. It starts with the basics— Bible reading and study, developing a prayer life, getting involved in a local church, and being a witness. When we gain victory in the basics, we will want more and God will want more from us. This is the sanctification—or spiritual growing—process we have discussed throughout this study.

Reread Joshua 14:6-15.
What is Caleb's "one-liner" testimony (vs. 8, 9, 14)?

What is Caleb's attitude about possessing the land?

Who were the Anakims (vs. 12; Numbers 13:27-33)?

While many of the tribes of Israel were slack to possess the land, we see a vastly different attitude in Caleb. He says, "Give me this mountain! I'll take on the giants!" He had waited years for this moment, and he was confident the LORD would be with him and help him drive out the Anakims. No doubt his confidence was directly related to his commitment to *wholly follow* the LORD.

What giants are you facing today?

How's your confidence in the LORD to help you defeat them?

Can you say you are wholly following the LORD and eager to possess the earthly inheritance you've been given?

Armour Up: Joshua 21:43-45

Arise, Go.

CHAPTER TWELVE
ARISE, GO.

Text: Joshua 22-24

In these final chapters, Joshua attempts to prepare Israel for continuing to live in victory. As their commander, he had safely led them in conquering the Promised Land. However, he knew the individual tribes had not succeeded in driving out all the inhabitants of the land and warned of the dangers of living among the other nations. Joshua wanted them to experience the great blessings the LORD had planned for them if they would walk in obedience to Him.

Don't Settle

The Eastern Tribes—the Reubenites, the Gadites, and the half tribe of Manasseh—had kept their commitment and helped Israel conquer the Promised Land. Now it was time for them to return to their inheritance. Joshua charges them with a charge that is still applicable to us today. He says in Joshua 22:5:

But take diligent heed to do the commandment and the law, which Moses the servant of the LORD charged you, to love the LORD your God, and to walk in all his ways, and to keep his commandments, and to cleave unto him, and to serve him with all your heart and with all your soul.

Underline the verbs (action words) in the passage above.
What does it mean to "take diligent heed"?

After Joshua charges the Eastern Tribes, he blesses them and sends them on their way. These two and a half tribes had been given the land of Gilead on the other side of Jordan. Their decision to settle there had caused some concern for Moses, and now the altar they built raised concerns among the other tribes.

Read Numbers 32. What was Moses's concern with their desire to settle in Gilead (vs. 6-15)?

What agreement did they make with Moses and the remaining tribes (vs. 16-23)?

What concerns did the Western Tribes have regarding the altar that was built (Joshua 22:15-20)?

What was the Eastern Tribes defense for building the altar (Joshua 22:22, 25-29)?

The building of the altar almost caused a civil war among the tribes. The Western Tribes were concerned the possession on the other side of Jordan was unclean and urged the two and a half tribes to pass over "unto the land of the possession of the LORD, wherein the LORD's tabernacle dwelleth" (Joshua 22:19). Even the Eastern Tribes themselves recognized the division the Jordan River created which motivated them to build the unnecessary altar (vs. 25).

God had already established memorials that would serve as reminders to their children. He had also set up a system of unified worship in which all the males were to gather in His chosen place (Shiloh at the time) three times a year. The building of the altar seemed to be a well-meaning act, but it "was the first of many by various tribes to fragment the unity of Israel" (Davis, 2008).

Lessons from the Eastern Tribes

1. Walk by faith, not by sight. One could argue that the Eastern Tribes focused on what they could see (a land good for cattle) rather than having faith in what awaited them across the Jordan. We must be careful not to get caught up in what this world has to offer, choosing instead to set our affection on things above (Colossians 3:1-2).

2. Distance leads to destruction. When we put distance between ourselves and the LORD, His House, and His people, we become easy targets for Satan to carry out his plans to destroy us. We must walk closely with the LORD and be present, active, and involved in our local churches.

3. Don't settle for anything less than God's best. The LORD wants us to live the Victorious Christian Life. He wants us to experience His exceeding great and precious promises. He wants us to walk in victory—over our own flesh, sin, and the enemy. We must not settle for anything less.

Cleave Unto the LORD

"And it came to pass a long time after that the LORD had given rest unto Israel…that Joshua waxed old and stricken in age" (Joshua 23:1). As Joshua approached the end of his earthly life, he called for all Israel to gather together. He reminded them of all they had seen and how the LORD had fought for them, warns them of the dangers of living among the idolatrous nations, and gives them some safeguards to protect themselves from falling away from the LORD.

Reread Joshua 23:6-16 and answer the following questions:

What encouragement and instruction does Joshua give in verse 6? How is this similar to Joshua 1?

What warnings did Joshua give regarding the other nations?

Why do you think it was important for the Israelites to be separated from the other nations? Why is it important for us to be set apart from this world?

What were they told to cleave to (vs. 8)?

Define cleave using Webster's 1828 dictionary.

What were they to "take good heed" to do (vs. 11)?

How does obedience, separation, and cleaving to the LORD protect us as we strive to live for the LORD?

Fear the LORD and Serve Him

Before we get into Joshua's final charge to the people, let's take a look at the significance of the place where he gathered the people for his last words. Shechem. This was the place where Joshua had read the words of the law, the blessings and cursings, to the congregation of Israel after their victory over Ai (Joshua 8). This was done to renew their covenant with the LORD, so it is a fitting place for Joshua to deliver his farewell address to the people (Hester, 2005).

What other events took place at Shechem (Genesis 12:6-7; 33:17-20; 35:1-4)?

Shechem had a history of being a significant place of spiritual decision. This gathering would be no different. Joshua reminds them of the LORD's promises and deliverance (Joshua 24:1-13) and then says, "Now therefore fear the LORD, and serve him in sincerity and in truth:" (vs. 14).

Take some time to look up the following words using Webster's 1828 Dictionary and the Strong's Concordance. Use what you learn to define the terms in your own words.

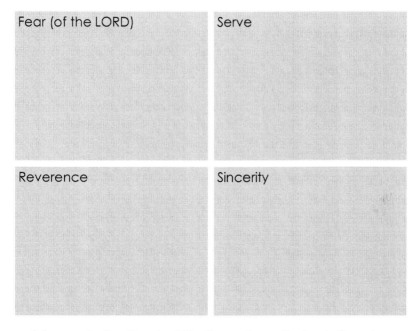

After reminding Israel of God's goodness, Joshua's first charge to the people is "fear the LORD." We cannot serve the LORD with a sincere heart unless we have a fear of the LORD, a proper reverence for Him. It is this fear mingled with respect and affection which produces a desire to serve and an unwillingness to offend Him (Webster's 1828).

Look up the following verses and take some notes about the fear of the LORD:

Psalm 111:10

Proverbs 9:10

Proverbs 14:26-27

Job 28:28

Ecclesiastes 12:13-14

There is an obvious connection between fearing the LORD and serving Him which is why Joshua said, "…fear the LORD, and serve him…" (24:14). It is our fear, or reverence, of the LORD that compels us to serve. When we have a healthy fear of the LORD, we know and understand Who God is and the power that He has over our lives. We surrender to His plan and purpose for our lives. We are willing to obey and worship as He commands.

Joshua goes on to say how they were to serve the LORD, "…in sincerity and in truth…" (vs. 14). Our service to the LORD should be sincere, our intentions and motivations pure and without hypocrisy. This requires continual self-examination. Am I truly surrendered to the Lord? Do I question His plans for my life? Am I willing to obey His commandments? What is my motivation for serving Him? The questions could continue, and our answers will probably vary from day to day. That is why we must be willing to check our hearts on a regular basis to ensure that we have a proper reverence for the Lord which prompts us to serve Him in sincerity and in truth.

Choose

Joshua brings his message to a point of decision. Serving the LORD in sincerity and in truth would cause the Israelites to put away all other gods. God had no interest in being included with their other gods. Exodus 34:14 says, "For thou shalt worship no other god: for the LORD, whose name is Jealous, is a jealous God:"

This brings us to probably one of the most popular Bible verses, often quoted and used to decorate Christian homes, Joshua 24:15:

And if it seem evil unto you to serve the LORD, choose you this day whom ye will serve; whether the gods which your fathers served that were on the other side of the flood, or the gods of the Amorites, in whose land ye dwell: but as for me and my house, we will serve the LORD.

Underline the portions of the verse above that you have heard or seen quoted most often.

More than likely, you noted "choose you this day whom ye will serve" and "as for me and my house, we will serve the LORD." I love both of those statements and have them up in my house in one room or another. It is what is sandwiched between them that is often overlooked: the call to put away other gods.

The people responded, "God forbid that we should forsake the LORD, to serve other gods" (vs. 16) and reaffirmed their commitment to serve the LORD (vs. 18, 21). They said the right words; they had good intentions. Unfortunately, we know the rest of the story. Good intentions without follow through will end in failure. We know the nation of Israel spiraled downward throughout the period of the Judges and "every man did that which was right in his own eyes" (Judges 21:25).

Read Judges 17:1-13 and consider Micah's misguided attempts to obtain the LORD's favor. What can we learn from this passage of Scripture?

Micah, his mother, and the hired Levite priest saw nothing wrong with taking money dedicated to the LORD to make graven images used to worship false gods. Micah had turned his home into a shrine unto false gods and mistakenly believed that because he had hired a Levite to be his priest in this unsanctioned place of worship, the LORD would bless him.

It's easy for us to see the problem with Micah's attempt to please God. It is more difficult for us to recognize the false gods and idols we have set up in our own lives. Our society has made it easy and even acceptable. We are encouraged to be consumed with self under the guise of "self-care," follow our heart, speak our truth, and do what feels right. All of this ungodly counsel is just one of Satan's sneaky tactics designed to get us to "do that which is right in our own eyes."

Consider the following questions:

- What money is being spent on the idols of this world that should be given to the LORD for tithes and offerings?

- How many are forsaking the assembly of themselves together to "worship" their family time, sports, nature, and hobbies?

- How many mistakenly believe that God will bless them because they believe in Him without making any attempt to follow His Word?

You may be thinking... *but I tithe and give to missions. I attend church every time the doors are open. I read my Bible and pray.* And that is all well and good, but what is our motivation for doing those things? What in our lives has taken too high a priority—becoming an idol? What areas of the Bible have we quietly ignored (i.e. witnessing, submitting to our husband, controlling our tongues, pride, bitterness, gluttony, etc.)?

Just as God demanded that Israel put away all other gods and serve Him alone, He demands the same from us. Jesus said the first and great commandment was that "Thou shalt love the Lord thy God with all thy heart, and with all thy soul, and with all thy mind" (Matthew 22:37). He knew that if our love for the LORD was our motivation, we would be willing to obey His Word and serve Him in sincerity and in truth. We would be willing to put away those things that distract, deter, or disallow us from serving the LORD and choose instead to follow Him with our whole hearts—holding nothing back.

Is there anything you need to "put away" so that you are able to serve the LORD in sincerity and in truth?

Read Joshua 24:24-27. What did Joshua do to commemorate the covenant the people made with God that day?

Arise and Go

"And it came to pass after these things, that Joshua the son of Nun, the servant of the LORD, died…" (Joshua 24:29). Joshua had fulfilled his mission as the commander of Israel. He had led his people to victory in conquering the Promised Land and possessing their earthly inheritance. And now it was time for him to receive his eternal inheritance.

What is Joshua's "one-liner" testimony in verse 29?

What happens to Israel (vs. 31; Judges 2:6-10)?

Israel served the LORD all the days of Joshua and the other elders which had "known all the works of the LORD" (vs. 31). Then there arose a generation after them which knew not the LORD, nor His works (Judges 2:10). It is easy to conclude that they failed to teach the children. But how could this happen? God had established several memorials to call to remembrance His mighty works on their behalf. How was it possible for them to forget the LORD's deliverance and all He had done for them?

They turned back (Psalm 78:54-58).

Don't misunderstand me. The Israelites continued to dwell in the Promised Land until the LORD allowed them to be taken into captivity as judgment for forsaking Him and serving other gods.

The nation of Israel *physically* stayed in the land of their possession, but *spiritually* they turned back to living in bondage and defeat.

I shared with you in the introduction that once I had crossed over into the Victorious Christian Life, I determined never to go back to the dry, empty Christian life I had been living. I still do not want to go back to going through the motions of Christianity—*physically* being in the "right place" while *spiritually* living in bondage and defeat. I want to continue walking in victory, enjoying sweet fellowship with my Savior, and experiencing true peace and everlasting joy. And I want the same for you.

It has been my prayer that as you have studied the book of Joshua, you have realized that you have everything you need to live a Victorious Christian Life. The Captain of your Salvation has equipped you for the spiritual battles you will face. Remember "the decisive blow has been struck at sin and Satan and the powers of darkness…and thereby the entire inheritance of 'all blessings in the heavenlies in Christ' is ours" (Hester, 2005). Choose to walk in victory. *Arise and go!*

Armour Up

Not ready for the study to end? It doesn't have to! The Bible is filled with the LORD telling people to "arise" or "rise" and… Use a Bible concordance to look up the words arise or rise and study the verses you find. Who is God commanding to arise or rise? What does He tell them to do next? How do they respond?

What can you learn from their response? Answering those questions and more will be an encouragement and challenge to your faith.

APPENDIX A
ABOUT ME

My husband and I are empty-nesters! We have two children, Chaz and Harley. They both graduated from Heartland Baptist Bible College in Oklahoma City and are seeking the LORD's direction in ministry.

Marc and I are active members of Temple Baptist Church in El Dorado, Kansas. He serves as a deacon and teaches the College and Career Sunday School class. We are both involved in the music ministries,

 although I always say, "I'm just making a joyful noise!" I also serve in various ladies' ministries around the church and help with our ladies' newsletter.

Writing for Him...has been my "tag line" since I started writing *many* years ago.

If you google me, you might even stumble on some inspirational fiction that I wrote in the past. Now, my focus is on devotions and Bible studies designed to encourage ladies in their walk with the Lord.

I was a stay-at-home mom when my kids were babies. When they started school, I went back to school and became a teacher. After spending time teaching 1st and 2nd grade, I am now an elementary reading specialist. I have also coached high school basketball and/or volleyball for many years. My hobbies include doing puzzles, exercising, reading, and writing.

I would love to connect with you, so please feel free to reach out to me.

Website: www.crystalratcliff.com

Facebook: https://www.facebook.com/authorcrystalratcliff/

Instagram: @authorcrystalratcliff

Email: crystal@authorcrystalratcliff.com

Crystal

APPENDIX B
MY SALVATION
TESTIMONY

I was raised in a Christian home. My parents took us to church every Sunday when I was little. I heard the salvation plan many times over the years. I even remember going forward one Sunday as a young child and talking to the pastor's wife. She showed me the salvation plan. I even remember the orange highlighted verses! However, as I grew older and my parents became even more involved in our church – we were now attending every time the doors were open – I began to have doubts about that salvation experience.

I didn't remember any *personal* conviction. I *did* remember that I had followed my older brother down the aisle. I prayed. I consulted my youth pastor's wife. You see, I was a very "good" girl. I was obedient to my parents. I didn't smoke, drink, or get involved with the wrong crowd. Everyone thought I was saved! So for awhile I bought into the lie that perhaps Satan was making me doubt my salvation to keep me from serving the Lord.

I am sad to say that this battle went on for several years. I was just too prideful to admit I wasn't saved. In many ways, I was relying on my service to get me to heaven. I was raised in church. I went to church every time the doors were open. I was active in my youth group. I was a "good" kid. Do you see how much emphasis was on "I"? Those years were miserable! I tried to *do* everything I was supposed to – read my Bible daily and pray, etc. – and I failed over and over again. There was no power in my life. I had not yet accepted Christ and could not possibly have victory over my sin.

God did not give up on me. Praise the Lord! He kept convicting me. And finally, the summer before my senior year of high school, I settled it. I sat in a youth camp service and listened as the preacher preached about hell, and I knew without a doubt that I was headed there. God truly broke my heart that day for my sin. I didn't see myself as a good kid; I saw myself for what I was – a sinner who needed salvation. My years of service didn't matter anymore. At this point, my thoughts changed to, "But everyone thinks I am already saved. What will they think of me if I admit that I'm not?" I decided that my pride was not going to cause me to spend an eternity in hell, and I accepted Christ as my Savior on July 12, 1995.

Have you accepted Christ as your Savior? It is the most important decision you will ever make, and I beg you to accept the free gift of salvation. Prayerfully consider the following verses and feel free to e-mail me if you have questions at crystal@authorcrystalratcliff.com.

For God so loved the world, that he gave his only begotten Son, that whosoever believeth in him should not perish, but have everlasting life. For God sent not his Son into the world to condemn the world; but that the world through him might be saved.

John 3:16-17

We are all sinners.

As it is written, There is none righteous, no, not one. There is none that understandeth, there is none that seeketh after God. They are all gone out of the way, they are together become unprofitable; there is none that doeth good, no, not one.

Romans 3:10-12

For all have sinned, and come short of the glory of God;

Romans 3:23

Wherefore, as by one man sin entered into the world, and death by sin; and so death passed upon all men, for that all have sinned:

Romans 5:12

We are hopelessly lost and have "earned" death (spiritual separation from God).

For the wages of sin is death; but the gift of God is eternal life through Jesus Christ our Lord.

Romans 6:23

Our hope is found in the gift of Jesus Christ *alone*.

But God commendeth his love toward us, in that, while we were yet sinners, Christ died for us.

Romans 5:8

That if thou shalt confess with thy mouth the Lord Jesus, and shalt believe in thine heart that God hath raised him from the dead, thou shalt be saved. For with the heart man believeth unto righteousness; and with the mouth confession is made unto salvation. For whosoever shall call upon the name of the Lord shall be saved.

Romans 10:9-10, 13

For by grace are ye saved through faith; and that not of yourselves: it is the gift of God: Not of works, lest any man should boast.

Ephesians 2:8-9

APPENDIX C
RECOMMENDED STUDY
SCHEDULE

I'm glad you have decided to study *Arise, Go*. I have included a sample schedule that can be used.

I tried to divide up the Scripture reading, study reading, and reflection questions in a way that would not require too much time from you each day. If you get behind, do NOT quit! Keep working even if it is at a slower pace. Use the weekends to catch up if needed.

You will notice that the Scripture reading is often repeated for multiple days or the duration of a specific chapter in the study. This is not a mistake. I have found that with multiple readings of the same passage, I'm giving the Lord more opportunities to speak to me and show me different lessons from the verses I may have previously missed.

It is my recommendation that you begin your study time with prayer and then read the text from the Bible. Please do not skip this part. There is power in the Word of God, not the word of Crystal Ratcliff. Also, be sure you pause while reading the study to look up the references that are sometimes given in parentheses. As you work through the study, allow plenty of time to prayerfully consider and answer the reflection questions. From personal experience, I know that I can often "skip" over a question thinking I'm "okay" only to have the Lord, through prayer, reveal to me that I still have some work to do in that specific area.

May the Lord bless you as you study His Word and seek a closer walk with Him!

		Week 1			
	MON	**TUE**	**WED**	**THU**	**FRI**
Scripture Reading	Joshua 1	Joshua 1	I Peter 5:5-11	Joshua 1	Eph. 6:10-18
Read and Do	**Intro. and Ch. 1** Meet the Captain (p. 1-3) Appendix A and B (optional)	**Ch. 1** The Captain of our Salvation (p. 4-8)	**Ch. 1** Armour Up: I Peter 5:5-11 (p. 8)	**Ch. 2** Keys to Success and The Armour of God (p. 11-13)	**Ch. 2** Cont. The Armour of God (p. 14-16)

		Week 2			
	MON	**TUE**	**WED**	**THU**	**FRI**
Scripture Reading	Eph. 6:10-18	Joshua 1	Psalm 19:7-11	Joshua 2	Joshua 2
Read and Do	**Ch. 2** Cont. The Armour of God (p. 17-20)	**Ch. 2** The Offensive Weapon (p. 20-22)	**Ch. 2** Armour Up: Psalm 19:7-11 (p. 22)	**Ch. 3** Deal with the Past (p. 25-28)	**Ch. 3** Rahab (p. 29-30)

137

	MON	TUE	WED	THU	FRI
Week 3					
Scripture Reading	II Samuel 22	I Timothy 1:12-17	Joshua 3	Joshua 3	Psalm 119:9-16
Read and Do	**Ch. 3** Cont. Rahab (p. 31-34)	**Ch. 3** Armour Up: I Timothy 1:12-17 (p. 34)	**Ch. 4** Sanctify Yourselves (p. 37-39)	**Ch. 4** Cont. Sanctify Yourselves (p. 40-42)	**Ch. 4** Armour Up: Psalm 119:9-16 (p. 42)
Week 4					
	MON	TUE	WED	THU	FRI
Scripture Reading	Joshua 3-4	Joshua 3-4	Hebrews 11	Joshua 3-4	Psalm 37:23-24; 18:30-36
Read and Do	**Ch. 5** Moving Forward (p. 45-48)	**Ch. 5** Elements of Faith (p. 48-50)	**Ch. 5** Examples of Faith (p. 51-52)	**Ch. 5** Encouragement of Faith (p. 53-55)	**Ch. 5** Armour Up: Psalm 37:23-24; 18:30-36 (p. 55)

Week 5					
	MON	**TUE**	**WED**	**THU**	**FRI**
Scripture Reading	Joshua 4	Joshua 4	Deut. 6:1-9	2 Peter 1:1-21	Joshua 5
Read and Do	**Ch. 6** Take Time to Remember (p. 57-59)	**Ch. 6** Crisis of Faith (p. 59-63)	**Ch. 6** Purpose of Memorials (p. 64-66)	**Ch. 6** Armour Up: 2 Peter 1:1-21 (p. 66)	**Ch. 7** Cutting Away (p. 69-71)
Week 6					
	MON	**TUE**	**WED**	**THU**	**FRI**
Scripture Reading	Joshua 5	Joshua 5	Col. 3:1-17	Joshua 6-8	Joshua 6-8
Read and Do	**Ch. 7** Christ our Passover (p. 72)	**Ch. 7** Cutting Away (p. 73-77)	**Ch. 7** Armour Up: Col. 3:1-17 (p. 77)	**Ch. 8** Victory and Defeat (p. 79-81)	**Ch. 8** From Victory to Defeat (p. 81-82)

139

Week 7					
	MON	**TUE**	**WED**	**THU**	**FRI**
Scripture Reading	Joshua 6-8	Romans 6	Joshua 9-10	Joshua 9-10	Joshua 9-10
Read and Do	**Ch. 8** Sin in the Camp Arise, Go, Do (p. 83-86)	**Ch. 8** Armour Up: Romans 6 (p. 87)	**Ch. 9** Beware of Satan's Attacks (p. 89-91)	**Ch. 9** Satan's Tactics (p. 91-92)	**Ch. 9** Fight Back (p. 93-95)

Week 8					
	MON	**TUE**	**WED**	**THU**	**FRI**
Scripture Reading	I Cor. 10:12-13	Joshua 10-14	Joshua 10-14	Joshua 10-14	II Kings 6:8-17
Read and Do	**Ch. 9** Armour Up: I Cor. 10:12-13 (p. 95)	**Ch. 10** The LORD Will Fight For You (p. 97-98)	**Ch. 10** The LORD Delivers (p. 99-100)	**Ch. 10** The LORD Defends Get in the Battle (p. 101-103)	**Ch. 10** Armour Up: II Kings 6:8-17 (p. 103)

Week 9					
	MON	**TUE**	**WED**	**THU**	**FRI**
Scripture Reading	Joshua 15-21	II Peter 1:1-11	Joshua 14	Joshua 21:43-45	Joshua 22 Numbers 32
Read and Do	**Ch. 11** Possess the Land Inheritance vs. Possession (p. 105-108)	**Ch. 11** Cont. Inheritance vs. Possession (p. 108-109)	**Ch. 11** Slack Not (p. 109-111)	**Ch. 11** Armour Up: Joshua 21:43-45 (p. 111)	**Ch. 12** Arise, Go Don't Settle (p. 113-116)

Week 10					
	MON	**TUE**	**WED**	**THU**	**FRI**
Scripture Reading	Joshua 22-24	Joshua 22-24	Joshua 22-24	Joshua 22-24	Your Turn
Read and Do	**Ch. 12** Cleave unto the LORD (p. 116-118)	**Ch. 12** Fear the LORD and Serve Him (p. 118-121)	**Ch. 12** Choose (p. 121-124)	**Ch. 12** Arise and Go (p. 121-126)	**Ch. 12** Armour Up (p. 126-127)

WORKS CITED

Baxter, J. S. (1976). *Explore The Book*. Grand Rapids, MI: Zondervan Publishing House.

Berg, J. (1999). *Changed into His Image*. Greenville: Bob Jones University Press.

Davis, J. J. (2008). *Conquest and Crisis*. Winona Lake: BMH Books.

Gaddis, J. (2018). Sin's Roll Call. Oklahoma City, OK, United States of America.

Hester, H. R. (2005). *Old Testament Bible History*. Blacktown: Missionary Outpost.

Ratcliff, C. L. (2016). *There's a Fly in my Tea! The Importance of Maintaining a Christian Testimony*. Rapid City: Crosslink Publishing.

Scofield, C. I. (1917). Scofield Reference Notes.

Spurgeon, C. H. (1882, January). *The Captain of our Salvation*. Retrieved from The Spurgeon Center: https://www.spurgeon.org/resource-library/sermons/the-captain-of-our-salvation/#flipbook/

Trotter, M. G. (2019). *52 Weeks of Pursuit*. Kansas City: Living Faith Books.

Wiersbe, W. W. (1993). *Be Available*. Colorado Springs: David C. Cook.

Wiersbe, W. W. (1993). *Be Strong*. Colorado Springs: David C Cook.

Made in the USA
Middletown, DE
09 September 2024

60611640R00088